Name and Image

THE ITALIAN LIST

ALSO FROM **THE ITALIAN LIST**

Edited by Alberto Toscano

Self-Portrait in the Studio
GIORGIO AGAMBEN
Translated by Kevin Attell

The Twilight of Politics
MARIO TRONTI
Translated by Matteo Mandarini

As Cruel as Anyone Else
ANGELO DEL BOCA
Translated by Richard Braude

Feminism in Revolt
CARLA LONZI
Edited by Luisa Lorenza Corna and Jamila M. H. Mascat
Translated by Luisa Lorenza Corna, Matthew Hyland, and Cristina Viti

The World Machine
PAOLO VOLPONI
Translated by Richard Dixon

Hamletics
MASSIMO CACCIARI
Translated by Matteo Mandarini

The Rain's Falling Up
LUCA RASTELLO
Translated by Cristina Viti

The Soul of Brutes
CARLO GINZBURG

The Idea of World
PAOLO VIRNO
Translated by Lorenzo Chiesa

Primo Levi
MARCO BELPOLITI
Translated by Clarissa Botsford

This Body That Inhabits Me
ROSSANA ROSSANDA
Translated by Richard Braude
Edited by Lea Melandri

The Golden Horde
Edited by NANNI BALESTRINI by
PRIMO MORONI
Translated by Richard Braude

Gianni Carchia

NAME AND IMAGE

An Essay on Walter Benjamin

TRANSLATED BY THOMAS HASKELL SIMPSON

LONDON NEW YORK CALCUTTA

This book has been translated thanks to a translation grant awarded by the Italian Ministry of Foreign Affairs and International Cooperation.

Questo libro è stato tradotto grazie a un contributo alla traduzione assegnato dal Ministero degli Affari Esteri e della Cooperazione Internazionale italiano.

Seagull Books, 2025

First published in Italian as
Nome e immagine. Saggio su Walter Benjamin

First published in English translation by Seagull Books, 2025

Paperback ISBN 978 1 80309 406 9

Hardback ISBN 978 1 80309 405 2

British Library Cataloguing-in-Publication Data
A catalogue record for this book is available from the British Library

Typeset by Seagull Books, Calcutta, India
Printed and bound by Hyam Enterprises, Calcutta, India

Non coerceri maximo,
contineri minimo, divinum est.

Not to be constrained by the greatest,
to be contained by the smallest, is divine.

—Epigraph for Hölderlin's *Hyperion.*

Contents

CHAPTER ONE

Criticism and Truth

1. On the relation between method and object in the philosophy of Walter Benjamin

An enlightening perspective seems to open up on this thinker if we attempt to imagine his physiognomic traits, aided by the memory of those who knew him. This is a permissible starting point, given the degree to which it extends one of the earliest and most characteristic motifs of Benjamin's thought: the determination of character as a mid-point between the Kantian ethical poles of nature and liberty, as outlined in the essay 'Fate and Character', composed in 1919 and published in 1921.[1] 'Character gives this mystical enslavement of the person to the guilt context the answer of genius.'[2] Physiognomy is one of the principal manifestations of this response. In this sense, the hermeneutic exercise which in the 'system of characterological signs is generally confined to the body,'[3] has been applied to Benjamin and seems to have become fixed in a formula by Adorno as the best way to introduce the discussion of his thought: 'Benjamin had something of the wizard about him, but

1 See the letter to Gerhard Scholem, dated 23 November 1919, in Walter Benjamin, *The Correspondence of Walter Benjamin, 1910–1940* (Manfred R. Jacobson and Evelyn M. Jacobson trans, Gershom Scholem and Theodor W. Adorno eds) (Chicago, IL: University of Chicago Press, 1994), p. 152.

2 Walter Benjamin, 'Fate and Character' in *Selected Writings* [*SW*], 4 VOLS (Marcus Bullock, Michael W. Jennings, Howard Eiland and Gary Smith eds) (Cambridge, MA: Harvard University Press, 1996–2003), VOL. 1: 1913–1926, p. 205. [All quotations in the present volume have been reproduced in British spelling for consistency. — Trans.]

3 Benjamin, 'Fate and Character' in *SW*, VOL. 1, pp. 201–2.

in a very literal, entirely non-metaphorical sense. Anyone could have imagined him with a very tall hat and a magic wand.' This image—a figural condensation of the meticulous list of physical details that accompany it—is paired up with the allusion of Benjamin's conceptual esotericism to the figure of the poker player, about whom Adorno notes that 'certain characteristics of his way of speaking and thinking were unquestionably not extraneous to Benjamin.'[4] Benjamin's philosophy does not allow itself to be reduced to categories; it is composite in its essence. 'Tirelessly the process of thinking makes new beginnings, returning in a roundabout way to its original object.'[5] It is not a philosophy of the concrete but starts from the concrete, mutating continuously in its development, in the encounter-conflict with whatever it tests itself against. There is no trace in it of any distinction between theme and development, thesis and result. The conception of dialectic in a state of stillness (*Stillstand*), a veritable backbone of Benjamin's approach, signifies nothing less than that the individual motifs of thought are all equally close to the centre (*Mittelpunkt*), all reciprocally harmonized and interwoven, without concern as to whether their succession forms a process of thought. The goal of communicating something or convincing the reader seems of no interest. Behind the laconic sign 'For Men' in 'One-Way Street' stands this teaching: 'To convince is to conquer without conception.'[6] However, if it is fundamental that philosophical representation become an authentic process of truth-discovery, it follows that a philosophy of this type is in its essence incapable of being presented. The primacy of the thing over the method reveals itself in the prohibition against expressing the principles from which to consequences are to be deduced. It is for this reason that, when introducing in 1955 the collection of his friend's writings, Adorno defined this philosophy with a term borrowed from modern

---

4 Theodor W. Adorno, 'Erinnerung' in Theodor W. Adorno, Ernst Bloch, Max Rychner, Gershom Scholem, Jean Selz, Hans Heinz Holz and Ernst Peter Fischer, *Über Walter Benjamin* (Frankfurt am Main: Suhrkamp, 1968), p. 12.

5 Walter Benjamin, *The Origin of German Tragic Drama* (John Osborne trans., George Steiner intro.) (London: Verso Books, 1998), p. 28.

6 Walter Benjamin, 'One-Way Street' in *SW*, VOL. 1, p. 446.

music: 'athematic'.[7] In intention, if not in result, this is an approach that will later orient Adorno's *Aesthetic Theory*:

> It is simply that from my theorem that there is no philosophical first principle, it now also results that one cannot build an argumentative structure that follows the usual progressive succession of steps, but rather that one must assemble the whole out of a series of partial complexes that are, so to speak, of equal weight and concentrically arranged all on the same level; their constellation, not their succession, must yield the idea.[8]

In Benjamin's atonality we grasp the sudden immobilization of movement into something static, the simultaneous presence in his thought of dialectic and non-dialectic elements.

The keystone of this philosophical method seems, then, to be the effort to capture the infinity of the philosophical object in the movement of the concept, in a dialectic 'that does not formally think through antithesis, but concretely, through differentiations'.[9] The concreteness Benjamin aims for is of an unusual type. He flees from any classificatory conceptual logic to seek refuge in the originary image of any hope whatever: the name of things and of mankind.

> This immediacy in the communication of abstraction came into being as judgment, when, in the Fall, man abandoned immediacy in the communication of the concrete—that is, name, and

---

7 Adorno's writings on Benjamin are collected in the volume *Über Walter Benjamin* (Frankfurt am Main: Suhrkamp, 1970). The citation is found on p. 46. English translation: Theodor W. Adorno, 'Introduction to Benjamin's *Schriften* (1955)' in Gary Smith (ed.), *On Walter Benjamin: Critical Essays and Recollections* (Cambridge, MA: MIT Press, 1988), pp. 2–17; here, p. 13. [Not to be confused with the 1968 publication of the same name, which features contributions from multiple authors, including Adorno. —Trans.]

8 Quoted in the Editors' Afterword to Theodor W. Adorno, *Aesthetic Theory* (Robert Hullor-Kentor trans., Gretel Adorno and Rolf Tiedmann eds) (London: Continuum, 1997), p. 364. The citation is from Adorno's correspondence, but the particular letter is not indicated by the editors.

9 Hans Heinz Holz, 'Prismatisches Denken' in Adorno et al., *Über Walter Benjamin* (1968), p. 65.

> fell into the abyss of the mediateness of all communication, of the word as means, of the empty word, into the abyss of prattle.[10]

This is an impulse encountered in the philosophical tendencies of the early twentieth century that arose in the search for the 'things in themselves' outside of their dead conceptual mould, against Kantian transcendentalism.

The immobilization of dialectic, which renounces the principle of foundation to bind itself intimately to the content of its object, can only take place in a specific sphere of thought. The 'will to power', the compulsion towards system, are inherent to a philosophical practice seized by a guilt complex when confronted by the ideal of indubitable certainty that belongs to science. The history of modern philosophy pivots around the problem inaugurated by Kant: How can metaphysics become a science? In this keeping with this intention, knowledge forgets its object, reducing it to a mere function of pre-constituted schemas and organizational moments. Such knowledge is in a hurry, admitting no tarrying with the phenomenon that would be capable of rendering it accessible. What distinguishes it is the demand for syllogistic continuity in the process of thought. And yet, 'the demand for flawless coherence in scientific deduction is not made in order that truth shall be represented in its unity and singularity; and yet this very flawlessness is the only way in which the logic of the system is related to the notion of truth.'[11] On the contrary, inconclusiveness pertains to authentic philosophical practice. Nothing in it can claim definitive validity, since the determination of the object necessitates repeated, innumerable additions and redefinitions. The apparent esoteric and poetic quality which Hegel considered characteristic of the beginning of any philosophy is maintained and strengthened in any course of thought that overflows the riverbanks of the system.[12] 'The alternative philosophical forms represented by the

---

10 Walter Benjamin, 'On Language as Such and On the Language of Man' in *SW*, VOL. 1, p. 72.

11 Benjamin, *The Origin of German Tragic Drama*, p. 33.

12 Georg Wilhelm Friedrich Hegel, *The Phenomenology of Spirit* (Terry Pinkard ed. and trans.) (Cambridge: Cambridge University Press, 2018), p. 10.

concepts of the doctrine and the esoteric essay are precisely those things which were ignored by the nineteenth century, with its concept of system.'[13] In Benjamin, rather than remaining abstract, this alternative was embodied in his epic, more than decade-long struggle around the *Pariser Passagen* (Paris Arcades). Responding to Adorno's perplexity with regard to the essay 'Paris, the Capital of the Nineteenth Century' (1935) and his praise for the 1929 draft of the *Arcades Project*,[14] Benjamin objected that the intentions contained in the first, original sketch admitted no structure except one that was illicitly 'poetic'.[15]

Formal exposition cannot be something secondary or extrinsic to philosophical thinking which aspires to truth. 'For knowledge, method is a way of acquiring its object—even by creating it in the consciousness; for truth it is self-representation, and is therefore immanent in it as form.'[16] An adequate principle of literary composition must be capable of expressing the representation of truth. 'The more clearly mathematics demonstrate that the total elimination of the problem of representation—which is boasted by every proper didactic system—is the sign of genuine knowledge, the more conclusively does it reveal its renunciation of that area of truth towards which language is directed.'[17] Wherever thinking philosophically is authentically a 'taking place' of philosophy, the truth can only be a process of moving along the path of its language, aimed at placing phenomena in such a light that they reveal on their own their reciprocal interconnections and secret structure. Ever since Benjamin's 1916 essay 'On Language as Such and on the Language of Man', this awareness expressed itself drastically:

> In God, name is creative because it is word, and God's word is cognizant because it is name [. . .] The absolute relation of name to knowledge exists only in God; only there is name,

---

13 Benjamin, *The Origin of German Tragic Drama*, p. 28.

14 See the letter dated 2 August 1935 to Benjamin, in *Correspondence*, pp. 494–503.

15 Letter to Gretel Adorno, 16 August 1935, in Benjamin, *Correspondence*, p. 507.

16 Benjamin, *The Origin of German Tragic Drama*, pp. 29–30.

17 Benjamin, *The Origin of German Tragic Drama*, p. 27.

> because it is inwardly identical with the creative word, the pure medium of knowledge [. . .] God rested when he had left his creative power to itself in man. This creativity, relieved of its divine actuality, became knowledge. Man is the knower in the same language in which God is the creator [. . .] All human language is only the reflection of the word in name. The name is no closer to the word than knowledge is to creation.[18]

Already in these words, allegory begins to take shape as the distinctive feature of Benjamin's philosophy, defining an approach to thought that can find its space exclusively in relation to pre-existing texts; that is, it can speak only because it listens. 'Truth is not a process of exposure which destroys the secret, but a revelation which does justice to it.'[19] The unresolvable allusiveness of this philosophical practice has its specific procedure—representation as 'peripeteia'—and its specific artistic genre: the essay or treatise.

'Representation as digression—such is the methodological nature of the treatise.'[20] The *Umweg*, the peripeteia, of representation is to be taken literally, and thus understood as the only means of preserving that constitutive allusiveness of philosophical practice. Only this allows the object to be understood not univocally but in the plurality of its meanings. *Umweg* (peripeteia) need not be understood as a roundabout way of drifting across the horizon of a bad infinity that rejects a rigorous sequence of thought. In the seven 'Principles of the Weighty Tome, or How to Write Fat Books', found under the heading 'Teaching Aid' in his 'One-Way Street', Benjamin himself derided such incapacity to immerse oneself into the heart of objects.[21] On the contrary, *Umweg* means closing in on an object that would slip away from any direct grasp, because in the face of truth, 'even the purest fire of the spirit of inquiry is quenched.'[22]

---

18 Benjamin, 'On Language as Such and On the Language of Man' in *SW*, VOL. 1, p. 68.

19 Benjamin, *The Origin of German Tragic Drama*, p. 31.

20 Benjamin, *The Origin of German Tragic Drama*, p. 28.

21 Benjamin, 'One-Way Street' in *SW*, VOL. 1, p. 457.

The circumnavigation of representation does not take as its motivation the search for the accessory, the derivative. Rather, it has its justification in dutiful respect for the transcendence of the truth. 'Truth is the death of intention. This, indeed, is just what could be meant by the story of the veiled image at Saïs, whose unveiling was fatal for whomsoever thought thereby to learn the truth.'[23] Benjamin's representational procedure requires instead 'the absence of an uninterrupted purposeful structure'[24] and its characteristics suit the treatise or essay, which aspire to a truth that goes against any system that posits itself as a sufficient systematization of formal knowledge. The constitutive essence of the treatise is not, in fact, the didactic diffusion of a specific knowledge, but rather the attempt, one might say, to go around the truth, which Benjamin knew to be inaccessible to autonomous reflection. The exercise of this authentic philosophical form,

> has imposed itself upon all those epochs which have recognized the un-circumscribable essentiality of truth in the form of a propaedeutic, which can be designated by the scholastic term treatise because this term refers, albeit implicitly, to those objects of theology without which truth is inconceivable. Treatises may be didactic in tone, but essentially they lack the conclusiveness of an instruction which could be asserted, like doctrine, by virtue of its own authority.[25]

The aphoristic quality Benjamin gives to this philosophical form in 'One-Way Street' reinforces its non-thematic ambiguity, categorized under the title 'Interior Decoration':

> The tractatus is an Arabic form. Its exterior is undifferentiated and unobtrusive, like the façades of Arabian buildings, whose articulation begins only in the courtyard. So, too, the articulated

---

22 Benjamin, *The Origin of German Tragic Drama*, p. 36.

23 Benjamin, *The Origin of German Tragic Drama*, p. 36.

24 Benjamin, *The Origin of German Tragic Drama*, p. 17.

25 Benjamin, *The Origin of German Tragic Drama*, p. 28.

> structure of the tractatus is invisible from the outside, revealing itself only from within. If it is formed by chapters, they have not verbal headings, but numbers. The surface of its deliberations is not enlivened with pictures, but covered with unbroken, proliferating arabesques. In the ornamental density of this presentation, the distinction between thematic and excursive expositions is abolished.[26]

The definition of the essay that Lukács had provided in his letter to Leo Popper, justifying the writings collected in *Soul and Form*, had already identified the exquisitely *allegorical* nature of this expositional form, but only barely touched upon its authentic reason for being in the necessarily indirect and mediated relation we entertain with truth. On the one hand, it grasps the irony that 'consists in the critic always speaking about the ultimate problems of life, but in a tone which implies that he is only discussing pictures and books.'[27] On the other, the autonomy of the essay as a genre is indeed recognized and guaranteed, but still as a moment within a hierarchical scale of functions, the final step of which remains the system: 'The essay can calmly and proudly set its fragmentariness against the petty completeness of scientific exactitude or impressionistic freshness; but its purest fulfilment, its most vigorous accomplishment, becomes powerless once the great aesthetic comes.'[28]

Prototypes of Benjamin's activity as a thinker are thus always only exercises similar to that of the interpreter, the translator, the critic. The rigorous limitation of his thought to what has already been formed by the spirit, to the document of culture—of which he reveals the complementary visage as 'document of barbarism'[29]—has the consequence of stiffening beneath his gaze the historical or human element in a sort of

---

26 Benjamin, 'One-Way Street' in *SW*, VOL. 1, p. 462.

27 György Lukács, *Soul and Form* (Anna Bostock trans., John T. Sanders and Katie Terazakis eds) (New York: Columbia University Press, 2010), p. 25.

28 Lukács, *Soul and Form*, p. 33.

29 Walter Benjamin, 'Eduard Fuchs, Collector and Historian' in *SW*, VOL. 3: 1935–1938, p. 267.

frozen natural world. As much in his analysis of the baroque world as in the later analysis of the relations within capitalist production, this theme of history as nature is unspoken but understood, as is, vice versa, the natural element as a secret prophecy of something authentically historical. In this way, in Adorno's words, 'all creation becomes writing to be deciphered, while the code is unknown.'[30] Benjamin's practice as essayist is configured in this way as a hermeneutic exercise whose model is the relationship of medieval commentators to the Bible. To treat profane texts as sacred scripture entails practising an interpretive activity whose ideal is the immersion of the text in the springwaters of prophetic meditation, its rebirth, which 'can only be achieved by recalling in memory the primordial form of perception.'[31] In fact, 'the specific historicity of works of art is likewise one that can be unlocked only in interpretations, not in "art history". For the process of interpretation brings to light connections between works of art that are timeless, yet not without a historical dimension.'[32]

2. Beyond transcendental philosophy

The theoretical presuppositions of Benjamin's work as an essayist, in parallel with his study of Jewish messianism, draw on Romantic propheticism, which constitutes the only angle from which he feels the philosophy of Romantic history can be seen.[33] Reflection on Jena Romanticism influenced Benjamin not only relative to its most easily recognizable derivation—criticism as the nucleus of philosophical practice, the only path to truth—but, more profoundly, such practice finds him in accord with a precise and all-encompassing conception of thought and history. Crucial elements of Benjamin's theory of language and epistemology already come to light in this regard. His interest turns to the

---

30 Adorno, *Über Walter Benjamin*, p. 41.

31 Benjamin, *The Origin of German Tragic Drama*, p. 36.

32 Walter Benjamin, 'Letter to Florence Christian Rang' in *SW*, VOL. 1, p. 389.

33 See the letter dated 7 April 1919 to Ernst Schoen, in Benjamin, *Correspondence*, pp. 139–40.

consideration of the Romantic philosophy of art as 'perhaps the greatest epoch in the philosophy of western art.'[34] His single goal is to contribute 'to an historical investigation into the problem [of] the concept of criticism in the transformations through which it has passed.'[35] But it is a fact that a full comprehension of this text was only rendered possible with the posthumous publication of his essay 'On the Program of the Coming Philosophy', whose drafting was contemporaneous with the writing of his graduate thesis.[36] The essay represents, in fact, the problematic setting from which the dissertation began its development. It reveals a paradoxical attempt to leave behind the aporias of transcendental philosophy by using methods taken from neo-criticism, in particular from the Marburg school and its founder, Hermann Cohen, who Benjamin esteemed especially in his double guise as a neo-Kantian philosopher and a scholar of Judaism. The term *metaphysics* here takes two meanings. It is employed, on the one hand, in a chastened Kantian guise, as a synonym for the 'structure of the knowledge of nature'. On the other, it appears as the possibility of a concept that evades those critical limits that in Kant alone define the constitution of knowledge as a system of nature. According to Benjamin, in this second meaning the term concerns 'the deducibility of the world from the supreme principle or nexus of knowledge—in other words, the concept of "speculative knowledge" in the precise sense of the term.'[37] Implicit here is a radical detachment from Kantianism, but Benjamin sees in this nothing other than his participation in 'the efforts of the neo-Kantian school directed towards the abolition of the strict distinction between the forms of intuition and the

---

34 Walter Benjamin, 'The Concept of Criticism in German Romanticism' in *SW*, VOL. 1, p. 175.

35 Benjamin, 'Concept of Criticism in German Romanticism' in *SW*, VOL. 1, p. 116.

36 The essay was published by Gershom Scholem for the first time in *Zeugnisse: Theodor W. Adorno zum 60. Geburstag* (Frankfurt am Main: Europäische Verlagsanstalt, 1963), preceded by a note stating that the author regards those pages as being of great importance.

37 This is a selection from the manuscript 'Über die Wahrnehmung'; Walter Benjamin, 'On Perception' in *SW*, VOL. 1, p. 94.

categories,' which he saw as beginning 'to discern the outlines of a development of the transcendental philosophy of experience into a transcendental or speculative philosophy.'[38] The singular contradiction of this latter formulation documents a decidedly equivocal reading of Cohen's work *Kants Theorie der Erfahrung* (Kant's Theory of Experience), which had just been published in its third edition and had become, according to Scholem's explicit testimony, the centre of Benjamin's meditations in this realm. Cohen is, in truth, absolutely distant from any attempt to interpret his effort to establish space and time as categories in a metaphysical rather than transcendental sense. In Cohen, rhe refusal of the Kantian distinction between intuition and thought has the sole purpose of establishing a logic of the origin (*Ursprung*) that banishes any derivation of thought from anything external.

The singularity of Benjamin's position consists in the fact that, for him, the difficulties and limits of Kantian epistemology are not immanent to it, but rather result from the degeneration and impoverishment imposed on metaphysics by Enlightenment thought, which left it incapable of covering the entire arc of possible experience. As the 'Program of the Coming Philosophy' argues,

> The very fact that Kant was able to commence his immense work under the constellation of the Enlightenment indicates that he undertook his work on the basis of an experience virtually reduced to a nadir, to a minimum of significance [. . .] Just what the lower and inferior nature of experience in those times amounts to, just where its astonishingly small and specifically metaphysical weight lies, can only be hinted at in the perception as to how this low-level concept of experience also had a restricting effect on Kantian thought. It is obviously a matter of that same state of affairs that has often been mentioned as the religious and historical blindness of the Enlightenment.[39]

38 Benjamin, 'On Perception' in *SW*, VOL. 1, p. 95.

39 Walter Benjamin, 'On the Program of the Coming Philosophy' in *SW*, VOL. 1, p. 101.

This notation can be found repeated at the beginning of the essay on 'Goethe's *Elective Affinities*': 'Kant's critical work and Basedow's *Treatise on the Elements*—the one dedicated to the meaning and the other to the perception of the experience of their times—testify in very different yet equally conclusive ways to the poverty of their material contents.'[40] In this sense, for Benjamin, 'the theory of the apriority of the two forms of intuition' is to be justified historically, in the sense that Kant used it in the attempt 'to separate [the concept of scientific experience] as far as possible from the ordinary meaning of experience' in his era.[41] Such a necessity has no reason to exist any longer if philosophy is now once again able to grasp the concept of an experience in which the science of nature is no longer a metaphysical question, but pertains rather, and quite literally, to a realm of experience beyond nature, intimately bound to theology. In this way, the cited passage leads to a claim that religion is 'presented' to philosophy as its 'object and content'.[42] This claim is wholly antithetical to the pure Neo-Kantian concept of thought, which cannot consent to anything, anywhere, being 'given' to thought, which is not synthesis, but production (*Erzeugung*).[43] Benjamin's intention to restore an integral concept of experience ('Experience as the object of knowledge is the unified and continuous manifold of knowledge')[44] is condensed into the proposition 'to create on the basis of the Kantian system a concept of knowledge to which a concept of experience corresponds, of which the knowledge is the teachings [*Lehre*].'[45]

The accusation made against the 'Program' that it falls back on mere criticism would stand only if the effort Benjamin called for had remained a simple 'evocation', as Rolf Tiedemann charges.[46] But it achieved a

---

40 Walter Benjamin, 'Goethe's *Elective Affinities*' in *SW*, VOL. 1, p. 298.

41 Benjamin, 'On Perception' in *SW*, VOL. 1, p. 94.

42 Benjamin, 'On the Program of the Coming Philosophy' in *SW*, VOL. 1, p. 109.

43 See Hermann Cohen, *System der Philosophie, Erster Teil: Logik der reinen Erkenntnis* (Berlin: Bruno Cassirer, 1914), pp. 35ff.

44 Benjamin, 'On Perception' in *SW*, VOL. 1, p. 95.

45 Benjamin, 'On the Program of the Coming Philosophy' in *SW*, VOL. 1, p. 108.

46 Rolf Tiedemann, *Studien zur Philosophie Walter Benjamin* (Frankfurt am Main: Suhrkamp, 1965), p. 12.

not-insignificant elaboration in the dissertation on the Romantics through the elaboration of the concept of art criticism. Benjamin was fully aware of this development:

> As soon as the history of philosophy, in Kant [. . .], still explicitly and emphatically affirmed both the possibility of thinking an intellectual intuition and its impossibility in the realm of experience, a manifold and almost feverish endeavour emerged to recover this concept for philosophy as the guarantee of its highest claims. At the forefront of this endeavour were Fichte, Schlegel, Novalis, and Schelling.[47]

We are not confronting here a collapse into a pre-critical position, but an attempt to overcome criticism in a productive, creative way. The reproach against Kant for his impoverishment of experience had already been canonical for speculative idealism in its various ramifications, but what is characteristic in Benjamin's recuperation of its motifs is the stark rejection of the Hegelian solution. The name Hegel appears only once in the entire dissertation,[48] in a passage where his dialectic is considered to be the complete and characteristic expression of the Fichtian dialectic of positing, that is, definitively freed from any mingling with the concept of reflection, which is instead the pole of the ambiguous Fichtian solution developed in all its implications by the Romantics. But the doubt which here is merely implied will be expressed quite drastically in a private communication: 'The Hegel I have read [. . .] has so far totally repelled me.'[49]

The revision of Kant that Benjamin entrusts to the coming philosophy applies not only on the side of experience and metaphysics. 'The weakness of the Kantian concept of knowledge has often been felt in the lack of radicalism and the lack of consistency in his teachings.'[50] The fact

---

47 Benjamin, 'Concept of Criticism in German Romanticism' in *SW*, VOL. 1, p. 121.

48 Benjamin, 'Concept of Criticism in German Romanticism' in *SW*, VOL. 1, p. 123.

49 Letter to Gerhard Scholem, 31 January 1918, in Benjamin, *Correspondence*, p. 112.

50 Benjamin, 'On the Program of the Coming Philosophy' in *SW*, VOL. 1, p. 102.

is that Kant has not found for knowledge 'the sphere of total neutrality in regard to the concepts of both subject and object', that 'autonomous, innate sphere of knowledge in which this concept in no way continues to designate the relation between two metaphysical entities.'[51] This lacuna has dramatic repercussions in the abyss created between apriority and the empirical, whereas it would be the responsibility of authentic knowledge to immerse itself so deeply into empirical experience as to be able to synthesize it, such that truth may be possible even for the fragile and the ephemeral:

> The problem faced by Kantian epistemology, as by every great epistemology, has two sides, and Kant managed to give a valid explanation for only one of them. First of all, there was the question of the certainty of knowledge that is lasting, and, second, there was the question of the integrity of an experience that is ephemeral. For universal philosophical interest is continually directed towards both the timeless validity of knowledge and the certainty of a temporal experience which is regarded as the immediate, if not the only, object of that knowledge. This experience, in its total structure, had simply not been made manifest to philosophers as something singularly temporal, and that holds true for Kant as well.[52]

Thus is already announced the great motif of the salvation of phenomena which is at the centre of the epistemological premise of *The Origin of German Tragic Drama* (*Ursprung des deutschen Trauerspiels*), which constitutes the true motor of all Benjamin's conceptual development.

Up to this point, the great result of Kant's work lies, for Benjamin, in having overcome the traditional characterization as object of the thing in itself as the cause of sensations, in having definitively dissolved any dogmatization of the entity as an objective substrate. Despite this, in Kant, 'there remains the subject nature of the cognizing consciousness

51 Benjamin, 'On the Program of the Coming Philosophy' in *SW*, VOL. 1, p. 104.

52 Benjamin, 'On the Program of the Coming Philosophy' in *SW*, VOL. 1, pp. 100–101.

to be eliminated,'[53] a nature that remains attached to the a priori synthetic judgments in the synthetic unity of apperception. This is so because, in Kantian epistemology, there has crept in

> a thoroughly metaphysical rudiment of epistemology [. . .] The most important of these elements are, first, Kant's conception of knowledge as a relation between some sort of subjects and objects or subject and object—a conception that he was unable, ultimately, to overcome, despite all his attempts to do so; and, second, the relation of knowledge and experience to human empirical consciousness, likewise only very tentatively overcome [. . .] This subject nature of this cognizing consciousness, however, stems from the fact that it is formed in analogy to the empirical consciousness, which of course has objects confronting it [. . .] It simply cannot be doubted that the notion, sublimated though it may be, of an individual living ego which receives sensations by means of its senses and forms its ideas on the basis of them plays a role of the greatest importance in the Kantian concept of knowledge.[54]

For Benjamin, Kantian rigor here mutates into mythology, which, in its truth content, is the exact equivalent of any other epistemological mythology, as we can find in peoples living in the state of nature or in mental alienation, in the paranormal states of the ill, and in seers. 'Cognizing man, the cognizing empirical consciousness, is a type of insane consciousness.'[55] It is a matter of undermining the hypostasis of the subject and situating the mission of the future epistemology in the recognition of the impossibility of an objective relation between any empirical knowledge and the objective concept of experience. This point of indifferentiation of knowledge, as intended by that 'sphere of total neutrality in regard to the concepts of both subject and object,'[56] is an announcement

---

53 Benjamin, 'On the Program of the Coming Philosophy' in *SW*, VOL. 1, p. 103.

54 Benjamin, 'On the Program of the Coming Philosophy' in *SW*, VOL. 1, p. 103.

55 Benjamin, 'On the Program of the Coming Philosophy' in *SW*, VOL. 1, pp. 103–4.

56 Benjamin, 'On the Program of the Coming Philosophy' in *SW*, VOL. 1, p. 104.

of what, according to the premise of the *Origin*, can only be defined as 'truth'—the setting in which ideas are located. 'Truth is an intentionless state of being, made up of ideas.'[57] It will be ideas that achieve the goal of the 'Program', to make them into 'a systematic specification of knowledge.'[58]

But already in his dissertation, before the prologue to the *Origin*, Benjamin had placed at the center of his interpretation that problem of indifferentiation which, inaugurated by the Romantics, finds in Schelling its most consequential theorist. At the same time he had attempted, on one hand, to posit an authentic experience against Kant's terribly impoverished one, and, on the other, to find a form of knowledge capable of avoiding the failed results of critical subjectivism.

3. Art criticism and knowledge

At the base of his exposition of the Romantic theory of knowledge, Benjamin posits the individuation of the paradoxical character of knowledge as carried out by Fichte in reference to reflection. 'Thinking that reflects on itself in self-consciousness is the basic fact from which Schlegel's and, in large part, Novalis' epistemological considerations take their start.'[59] Thought and reflection are identified because in the reflective nature of thought one finds a guarantee for its intuitive character. But if we also find in this identification a complete convergence between the Romantics and Fichte's position, the Romantics do not content themselves with the immediacy of knowledge that this 'radical mystical formalism'[60] guarantees. In fact, the concept of reflection seems equally able to offer a singular infinity of the cognitive process, a peculiar inconclusiveness. Where Fichte's labours seem totally directed towards excluding from theoretical philosophy the infinity of the action of the ego in order to

57 Benjamin, *The Origin of German Tragic Drama*, p. 36.

58 Benjamin, 'On the Program of the Coming Philosophy' in *SW*, VOL. 1, p. 103.

59 Benjamin, 'Concept of Criticism in German Romanticism' in *SW*, VOL. 1, p. 120.

60 Benjamin, 'Concept of Criticism in German Romanticism' in *SW*, VOL. 1, p. 123.

channel it exclusively into the practical, 'the Romantics seek to make it constitutive precisely for theoretical philosophy and thus for philosophy as a whole.'[61] But if the Romantics found no obstacle in that infinity of reflection against which Fichte was erecting imposing barriers, this is because of the fact that reflection—with its thinking about thinking about thinking, and so on—was for them anything but a banal sequencing of empty, endless thoughts. Benjamin's observation is decisive: 'The infinity of reflection, for Schlegel and Novalis, is not an infinity of continuous advance but an infinity of connectedness.'[62] The construction of the schema of Romantic epistemology on the basis of this infinity of relation, a circular process of mediation through immediacies, constitutes itself in the sense of the derivation of each level of reflection from the previous one, in a spontaneous manner, as its self-knowing. As Schlegel observes, 'Sense that sees itself becomes spirit.'[63] The differences from Fichte are again determinative here, because whereas for him, 'a self belongs only to the "I"—that is, a reflection exists only and uniquely in correlation with a position'[64]—Romantic reflection relates to mere thinking, and what is verified there in a single case takes place instead continuously in Romantic intuition. According to Schleiermacher's formulation, 'Self-intuition and intuition of the universe are reciprocal concepts; for this reason, every reflection is infinite.'[65] The Romantic absolute thus takes form as a 'medium' of reflection. 'With this term, one may characterize the whole of Schlegel's theoretical philosophy.'[66] In this medium, any simple reflection arises absolutely from a point of indifferentiation that must be determined. The Romantics understood this *Mittelpunkt* as the domain of art, and this latter now seems to present

---

61 Benjamin, 'Concept of Criticism in German Romanticism' in *SW*, VOL. 1, p. 123.

62 Benjamin, 'Concept of Criticism in German Romanticism' in *SW*, VOL. 1, p. 126.

63 Cited in Benjamin, 'Concept of Criticism in German Romanticism' in *SW*, VOL. 1, p. 127.

64 Benjamin, 'Concept of Criticism in German Romanticism' in *SW*, VOL. 1, p. 128.

65 Benjamin, 'Concept of Criticism in German Romanticism' in *SW*, VOL. 1, 132.

66 Benjamin, 'Concept of Criticism in German Romanticism' in *SW*, VOL. 1, p. 132.

itself to Benjamin as that higher realm of experience whose necessity the 'Program' underscored. Benjamin seems to find here—in the creative omnipotence of reflection, in the poetic sentiment which, spurting up from nothingness, reveals itself as reflection's point of indifferentiation—that supersession of the 'mechanical' experience of transcendental philosophy which the 'Program' generically indicated with the term 'religious' experience.[67]

In the final pages of his dissertation, Benjamin finds it necessary to preface his explication of the idea of this sphere with an account of its appropriate cognitive instrument: art criticism. This explanation too, however, demands a more radical justification. 'Criticism comprises the knowledge of its object. For this reason, an exposition of the early Romantic concept of the criticism of art requires a characterization of the theory of the knowledge of objects, on which that concept is based.'[68] This theory embraces, on one hand, the field of natural objects, on the other, that of works of art. Unfolding the concept of reflection reveals that all that is in the absolute thinks, but since this thought is reflection, it can think only of itself.

> All knowledge is self-knowledge of a thinking being, which does not need to be an 'I'. Moreover, the Fichtean 'I', which is set in opposition to the 'not-I', to nature, signifies for Schlegel and Novalis only an inferior form among an infinite number of forms of the self. For the Romantics, from the standpoint of the absolute, there is no 'not-I', no nature in the sense of a being that does not become itself.[69]

The rootedness of any knowledge of the object in a self-knowledge of the object itself is expressed in the most paradoxical form in Novalis's brief proposition, 'Perceptibility [is] an attentiveness,'[70] which Benjamin

---

67 Benjamin, 'On the Program of the Coming Philosophy' in *SW*, VOL. 1, 105.

68 Benjamin, 'Concept of Criticism in German Romanticism' in *SW*, VOL. 1, p. 143.

69 Benjamin, 'Concept of Criticism in German Romanticism' in *SW*, VOL. 1, p. 145.

70 Benjamin, 'Concept of Criticism in German Romanticism' in *SW*, VOL. 1, p. 145.

repeated in his essay on Baudelaire in terms of the notion of aura.[71] The question of the relation between subject and object in knowledge, which from a critical orientation led to the reciprocal hardening of two opposed metaphysical entities, here instead seems to be heading towards a solution, in the sense that no knowledge of an object comes through a subject, but rather within a 'medium' consisting of reflection. The thing and the knowing essence pass into one another. We encounter here an acquisition which, although announced in the 1916 writings on language, is now further detailed and articulated into a series of theoretical perspectives that Benjamin will continue to utilize. This context is the origin, at great remove, of one of the most significant thoughts in the final work that Benjamin would put his hand to: the illustration of a concept of labour which, 'far from exploiting nature, would help her give birth to the creations that now lie dormant in her womb,' as expressed in the theses of 'On the Concept of History'.[72] The same solution is found in the dissertation, in fact, for the question of the knowledge of the natural object or, in different terms, for that of observation and experiment. The conduct of the researcher must be guided by the awareness that no knowledge is possible without the self-knowledge of that which *is* to be known, which is to say that observing a thing must mean only arousing it to its own self-knowledge. In this sense, Novalis claimed of the authentic experimenter that nature 'reveals itself all the more completely through him, the more his constitution is in harmony with her', such that 'the process of observation is at the same time a subjective and objective process, an ideal and a real experiment.'[73] That Benjamin is extremely close to this conception is demonstrated by the attention he dedicated to Goethe's concept of the *empiria*, which is contiguous with the Romantic concept of the observation of nature. This is especially the case with the annotation according to which everything factual is already

71 Walter Benjamin, 'On Some Motifs in Baudelaire' in *SW*, VOL. 4: 1938–1940, p. 338.

72 Walter Benjamin, 'On the Concept of History' in *SW*, VOL. 4, p. 394.

73 Benjamin, 'Concept of Criticism in German Romanticism' in *SW*, VOL. 1, p. 148.

theory, as expressed in this proposition: 'There is a tender empiria that conforms intimately to its object and that, through identification with it, becomes its true and proper theory.'[74]

If art is the determination of the 'medium' of reflection richest in consequences that Romanticism was able to conceive of, then art criticism positions itself as the necessary knowledge of the object within this 'medium'. 'The task for the criticism of art is knowledge in the medium of reflection that is art,'[75] which establishes a relation with the work of art according to the same laws that regulate observation of the natural object. That which in this last case was opposition to the tyrannical domination of nature exercised in the name of scientific absolutism, reveals itself here as a refusal to submit the work of art to a judgement whose metric is not immanent to it. Benjamin's interest in this Romantic theory is anything but archaeological: 'Thus, in complete antithesis to the present-day conception of its nature, criticism in its central intention is not judgement but, on the one hand, the completion, consummation, and systematization of the work and, on the other hand, its resolution in the absolute.'[76] In this vision, criticism posits itself as an experiment in the work of art through which the work itself must be reawakened to its reflection, and thus led to knowledge and to its self-knowledge. 'Insofar as criticism is knowledge of the work of art, it is its self-knowledge; insofar as it judges the artwork, this occurs in the latter's self-judgment.'[77] This, however, is a particular judgement in which the negative moment—at base, that which from outside wishes to impose its dominion—has a disproportionately small role. What counts, in fact, is the completely positive moment of the elevation of knowledge in the reflecting person, by which this criticism 'is radically distinguished from the modern concept, which sees criticism as a negative court of judgement.'[78]

74 This is observation 575 of Goethe's *Maximen und Reflexionem* (1833). Cited in Benjamin, 'Concept of Criticism in German Romanticism' in *SW*, VOL. 1, p. 192n149.

75 Benjamin, 'Concept of Criticism in German Romanticism' in *SW*, VOL. 1, p. 151.

76 Benjamin, 'Concept of Criticism in German Romanticism' in *SW*, VOL. 1, p. 159.

77 Benjamin, 'Concept of Criticism in German Romanticism' in *SW*, VOL. 1, p. 151.

78 Benjamin, 'Concept of Criticism in German Romanticism' in *SW*, VOL. 1, p. 152.

But if, for the Romantics, 'criticism is far less the judgement of a work than the method of its consummation,'[79] it follows that 'it is an art and not a science'[80]—and in effect the Romantics have removed any distinction between criticism and poetry. This is not an overcoming of rationalism in the sense of an unlimited cult of the creative force, 'as so many modern authors, following the train of their own thinking, have misunderstood.'[81] Rather, the new meaning that the term 'criticism' assumes in this context is entirely characteristic. As regards the theory of art, in fact, the Romantics had the impression of finding themselves in a problematic situation analogous to that of Kant in the field of epistemology. It was necessary, on the one hand, to make a breach in the dogmatism of those who wanted to subject the work of art to a judgement fixed in external laws; on the other, it was also necessary to defeat the scepticism of Sturm und Drang, with its cult of unruly genius. But beyond the faint echo of Kantian influence, the term 'criticism' had by now acquired a distinctly speculative meaning, standing for 'objective', 'productive' and 'creative through reflection'.

Freedom from heteronomous aesthetic doctrines is obtained by fixing a criterion of the work of art different from the rule, that is, the criterion of a determinate structure immanent to the artwork itself. The correlative of such a concept of criticism can therefore only be a clearly determined concept of the work. For the Romantics, such a concept is expressed in the theory of its form, which is nothing other than 'the objective expression of the reflection proper to the work' and which, as 'the possibility of reflection in the work [. . .] grounds the work a priori, therefore, as a principle of existence: it is through its form that the work of art is a living centre of reflection.'[82] This overcoming of the principle of dogmatic rationalism in aesthetics is expressed most clearly in a proposition of Novalis, according to which, 'Every work of art has an a priori

79 Benjamin, 'Concept of Criticism in German Romanticism' in *SW*, VOL. 1, p. 153.

80 Lukács, *Soul and Form*, p. 17.

81 Benjamin, 'Concept of Criticism in German Romanticism' in *SW*, VOL. 1, pp. 154–55.

82 Benjamin, 'Concept of Criticism in German Romanticism' in *SW*, VOL. 1, p. 156.

ideal, an intrinsic necessity, to exist.'[83] The full weight of this statement can be understood by the fact that Benjamin frequently returned to it during the early phase of his thought, in the essay on Hölderlin,[84] in the one on Dostoevsky,[85] and yet again in the prologue to his work on German tragic drama.[86]

Decisive for Benjamin, in the type of reading the Romantics practice on works of art, is the fact that it is a form of exegesis that does not eliminate the artwork, since the work does not need any founding justification, any reductive motivation. 'Romantic theory grounds the validity of forms independently of the ideal of determinate structures,'[87] and does this to the extent that it gives itself a structure in which 'form did not count [. . .] either as a rule in itself or even as dependent on rules.'[88]

Benjamin expresses in three principles the consequences which, in any theory of judgement, result from this reflection, by which the criticism of an artwork is its own self-reflection, the full unfolding of its immanent germ. What must count above all is the axiom that the value of the artwork depends exclusively upon its rendering more or less possible the criticism immanent to itself, which is to say 'the criticizability of a work demonstrates on its own the positive value judgement made concerning it.'[89] If any judgement of works of art must have implicit value, it goes without saying that judgement may possess no positive scale of values, and as an extreme consequence, the principle must prevail that what is no good cannot be criticized. This conception, which utterly vanquishes the Enlightenment rationalism fixed on squeezing the work of art into the narrow function of a means for the exposition of a content, is also the only one that permits us to approach the work of art with a

---

83 Benjamin, 'Concept of Criticism in German Romanticism' in *SW*, VOL. 1, p. 158.

84 Walter Benjamin, 'Two Poems by Friedrich Hölderlin' in *SW*, VOL. 1, p. 19.

85 Walter Benjamin, 'Dostoevsky's *The Idiot*' in *SW*, VOL. 1, p. 79.

86 Benjamin, *The Origin of German Tragic Drama*, p. 52.

87 Benjamin, 'Concept of Criticism in German Romanticism' in *SW*, VOL. 1, p. 158.

88 Benjamin, 'Concept of Criticism in German Romanticism' in *SW*, VOL. 1, p. 158.

89 Benjamin, 'Concept of Criticism in German Romanticism' in *SW*, VOL. 1, p. 160.

genuine wish to listen and come to it, with dutiful care not to superimpose the subjective will of the interpreter upon the real intentions of the artistic fact.

> Criticism, which for contemporary understanding is the most subjective of things, was for the Romantics the regulator of all subjectivity, contingency, and arbitrariness in the genesis of the work [. . .] the distinctive element of the Romantic concept of criticism lies in its freedom from any special subjective estimation of the work in a judgement of taste. Valuation is immanent to the objective investigation and knowledge of the work.[90]

In this light it is necessary to reconsider the concept of irony, which seems, in common opinion, to constitute a fundamental objection to this full-blown demand for respect towards the work of art. It is to the credit of Benjamin the philologist to have put into relief the deformation introduced into philosophical historiography by the unilateral interpretation of irony as the expression of a pure subjectivism.

Certainly, there exists for the Romantics a subjectivist irony whose spirit is expressed in the figure of the author who rises disdainfully above the materiality of the work, but this comes from the author's will to establish the material as the only field of play, while 'the objective lawfulness to which the artwork is subjected by art consists, as has been noted, in the form of the work.'[91] The opinion regarding Romantic subjectivism arose to the degree that there was a failure to discern in irony, which invests the poetic form, something completely different from the ironization of the material, because 'the latter rests on a demeanour of the subject; the former presents an objective moment in the work itself.'[92] This type of formal irony presents great affinities with the objective aspiration in art, which is criticism. In keeping with one of the tasks of criticism, the more rigorous the form of the artwork, the more intensely

---

90 Benjamin, 'Concept of Criticism in German Romanticism' in *SW*, VOL. 1, pp. 160–61.

91 Benjamin, 'Concept of Criticism in German Romanticism' in *SW*, VOL. 1, p. 162.

92 Benjamin, 'Concept of Criticism in German Romanticism' in *SW*, VOL. 1, p. 163.

criticism must attempt to resolve the individual artwork into the absolute work of art, by 'romanticizing it' (to use Novalis's expression) in the idea of art itself. In the same way, formal irony originates in reference to the unconditional. It is not a matter of subjectivism and play, 'but of the assimilation of the limited work to the absolute, of its complete objectivization at the price of its ruin.'[93] Whereas the irony of the material is negative and subjective, that of the form is positive and objective. But the authentic positivity of this formal irony marks at the same time its moment of differentiation from criticism, which also aims at achieving objectivity. Whereas criticism, in the interest of a higher unity of art and philosophy, does not hesitate to sacrifice the single work of art, formal irony is capable of maintaining the work's integrity while at the same time drawing it into to the idea of art.

> The particular form of the individual work, which we might call the presentational form, is sacrificed to ironic dissolution. Above it, however, irony flings open a heaven of eternal form, the idea of forms (which we might call the absolute form), and proves the survival of the work, which draws its indestructible subsistence from that sphere, after the empirical form, the expression of its isolated reflection, has been consumed by the absolute form.[94]

Benjamin discerns in the concept of the idea of art the authentic crowning of the various Romantic theorems of criticism, the artwork and irony. While the entire argument had started with the determination of the absolute 'medium' of reflection as art, once the organ of artistic reflection has been defined as form, the idea of art qualifies as the 'medium' of reflection of the forms. In this way, reflection comes to demonstrate a process *toto caelo* different from the subjective reflective procedure of the Kantian faculty of judgment. Reflection, in fact, remains enclosed in the form of representation of the artwork, awaiting only to be unfurled

---

93 Benjamin, 'Concept of Criticism in German Romanticism' in *SW*, VOL. 1, p. 164.

94 Benjamin, 'Concept of Criticism in German Romanticism' in *SW*, VOL. 1, p. 164.

through criticism and brought to its ultimate fulfilment in the *continuum* of forms. One must guard against misunderstanding the idea of this *continuum* as an abstraction from empirically encountered works of art. As will be stated in the *Origin*, 'It is the function of concepts to group phenomena together.'[95] But what Schlegel and the Romantics are after is the expression of the supreme universal as true and actual individuality, that is, the expression of the unity of art as an idea in the Platonic sense, as the real foundation of any empirical artwork. In the *continuum* of forms, Benjamin explains, 'for the evolving unity of poetry, as for the unity of the invisible work, the equalization and reconciliation of forms is the visible and authoritative process. Ultimately the mystical thesis [is] that art itself is an artwork.'[96]

'Romantic poetry is a progressive universal poetry . . . The Romantic way of writing is still in the process of becoming; indeed, this is its proper essence—that it is eternally coming to be and can never be completed.'[97] Benjamin begins from this celebrated aphorism of Friedrich Schlegel to then introduce several decisive clarifications. He puts us on guard against the danger of falling into the modernizing equivocation which consists in understanding infinite progression 'as a mere function of the indeterminate infinite of the task, on the one hand, and the empty infinity of time on the other.'[98] Schlegel's universal progressive poetry achieves its task only in the determinate, in the individuality of ideas and temporal infinity in which this progress takes place; not in an empty, abstract infinity, but rather in one that is medial and qualitative. The polemic against the empty time of historicism found in the theses 'On the Concept of History' is already implicit in the dissertation: 'progredibility [*Progredibilität*] is not at all what is understood by the modern term "progress"; it is not some merely relative connection of cultural

95 Benjamin, *The Origin of German Tragic Drama*, p. 35.

96 Benjamin, 'Concept of Criticism in German Romanticism' in *SW*, VOL. 1, p. 167.

97 Benjamin, 'Concept of Criticism in German Romanticism' in *SW*, VOL. 1, p. 168.

98 Benjamin, 'Concept of Criticism in German Romanticism' in *SW*, VOL. 1, p. 168.

stages to one another. Like the entire life of mankind, it is an infinite process of fulfilment, not a mere becoming.'[99]

It's not a matter here of an arbitrary coming together of the two extremes of Benjamin's creative arc, because their conceptual affinity shares a terminological correspondence too precise to be considered casual or forced. 'The historical materialist cannot do without the notion of a present which is not a transition, but in which time takes a stand [*einsteht*] and has come to a standstill.'[100] We should return here to the original text: '*Auf den Begriff einer Gegenwart, die nicht Übergang ist, sondern in der Zeit einsteht und zum Stillstand gekommen ist, kann der historische materialist nicht verzichten*.'[101] The term *Stillstand* was used by Schlegel in the *Lucinde*, and Benjamin cites the passage containing the word in his dissertation. It is not by chance that the word precisely refers to the Romantic polemic against the ideology of progress: 'What, then, is the purpose of this unconditioned striving and advancing without cessation [*Stillstand*] or centrepoint [*Mittelpunkt*]? [. . .] It is nothing more, this empty restless forcing, than a Nordic vice.'[102] This coincidence is enlightening and quite deserving of attention, despite having been distinctly ignored by previous interpreters.

It is not by chance that 'cyclic' philosophy is the heading under which Schlegel, in the fragments published by Windischmann,[103] categorized his representation of the philosophical system. This was in conformity with his refusal of any dialectic triggered and proceeding in an indeterminate sense. The question of the system is the point where the

---

99 Benjamin, 'Concept of Criticism in German Romanticism' in *SW*, VOL. 1, p. 168.

100 Benjamin, 'On the Concept of History' in *SW*, VOL. 4, p. 396.

101 Walter Benjamin, 'Über den Begriff der Geschichte' in *Gesammelte Schriften*, 7 VOLS (Frankfurt am Main: Suhrkamp, 1972–1991), VOL. 1, TOME 2, p. 702.

102 Benjamin, 'Concept of Criticism in German Romanticism' in *SW*, VOL. 1, p. 169; in Friedrich Schlegel, 'An Idyll of Idleness' in '*Lucinde*' *and the Fragments* (Peter Firchow trans. and intro.) (Minneapolis, MN: University of Minnesota Press, 1971), p. 29.

103 See Friedrich Schlegel, *Philosophische Vorlesungen* (*1800–1807*) (Jean-Jacques Anstett ed.) (Munich / Paderborn / Vienna: Schoningh, 1964), VOLS 12 and 13.

conception of criticism and the work of art that Benjamin is focused on in the Romantic tradition shows itself best in its quality as a response to the unresolvability charged by any Kantian (and Neo-Kantian) approach. The drafting of the text on the 'Program' saw Benjamin still convinced of the possibility of a system of philosophy. His aim is the revision and continuance of the Kantian system on a path that leads philosophy to configure itself as doctrine.[104] But the dissertation puts this perspective into crisis, no matter how ambiguous the way out of the problem indicated here. The Kantian effort to grasp the absolute systematically is opposed to the example of Friedrich Schlegel who, turning the terms upside down, wants to grasp the system in an absolute manner.

> Certainly, for Friedrich Schlegel in the 'Athenaeum' period, the absolute was the system in the form of art. Rather than attempting to grasp the absolute systematically, however, he sought conversely to grasp the system absolutely. This was the essence of his mysticism and [. . .] the perilous character of this venture did not remain hidden from him.[105]

There is no need to read these last words as a critique of Schlegel's formulation, but rather a reproach directed at a misunderstanding, an inconsequentiality within a line of thought that is otherwise adequate. That 'perilous element' consists not in the 'absolutist' claims of the effort, but rather in its aim towards the end goal of a 'system' which by definition eludes, according to Benjamin, any direct conceptual grasp. Schlegel's misunderstanding is above all a matter of terminology which, as far as concerns the characteristics of his 'mystical' philosophy, could be repeated virtually word for word by Benjamin.

In the dissertation, however, the answer to the problem of the system effectively remains entrusted to the intuition of the interpreter, concealed as it is beneath the veil of an indirect, mediated exposition. The solution

---

104 See the letter to Gerhard Scholem, 22 October 1917, in Benjamin, *Correspondence*, p. 97ff.

105 Benjamin, 'Concept of Criticism in German Romanticism' in *SW*, VOL. 1, p. 138.

proposed by Benjamin in the essay on 'Goethe's *Elective Affinities*' and in the prologue to the book on German tragic drama allows us to bring retrospective illumination to the issue raised by Schlegel.

The formula 'ideal of the problem' is often used here as a substitute for the term 'system', but nothing has changed as to its content.

> The totality of philosophy, its system, is of a higher magnitude of power than can be demanded by the quintessence of all its problems taken together, because the unity in the solution of them all cannot be obtained by questioning. If, that is to say, it were possible to obtain the very unity in the solution to all problems as the answer to a question, then with respect to the question seeking this unity, a new question would immediately arise, on which the unity of its answer together with that of all the others would be founded. It follows that there is no question which, in the reach of its inquiry, encompasses the unity of philosophy. The concept of this nonexistent question seeking the unity of philosophy by inquiry functions in philosophy as the ideal of the problem.[106]

It is typical that, in the prologue to the *Origin*, there is an entirely similar argument concerning the transcendental unity of the truth: 'Knowledge is open to question, but truth is not. [. . .] unity is present in truth as a direct and essential attribute, and as such it is not open to question.'[107] Only an allusive, allegorical process is capable of grasping the ideal of the problem, and this finds its concretization in works of art. 'Even if, however, the system is in no sense attainable through inquiry, there are nevertheless constructions which, without being questions, have the deepest affinity with the ideal of the problem. These are works of art.'[108] This is to say that the unity of philosophy (and, we can say, also of truth) not only cannot be grasped by philosophy itself, but philosophy cannot

---

106 Benjamin, 'Goethe's *Elective Affinities*' in *SW*, VOL. 1, pp. 333–34.

107 Benjamin, *The Origin of German Tragic Drama*, p. 30.

108 Benjamin, 'Goethe's *Elective Affinities*' in *SW*, VOL. 1, p. 334.

even pose itself the question. Thus arises Benjamin's charge regarding Schlegel's incoherence. Because if this unity is realized in works of art, then it becomes accessible to that which is the supreme Romantic discovery: criticism as revelation of the truth of a work of art. The ideal of the problem, according to a law founded in its essence itself, 'can represent itself solely in a multiplicity.'[109] As a principle, the unity of philosophy can be known only in a plurality and multiplicity of virtual questions.

> The ideal of the problem, however, does not appear in a multiplicity of problems. Rather, it lies buried in a manifold of works, and its excavation is the business of critique. The latter allows the ideal of the problem to appear in the work of art in one of its manifestations.[110]

Benjamin's point of arrival here is not the pure and simple liquidation of the system, as might appear to be the case, especially given the fragmentary nature of his work. With explicit and symptomatic reference to Nietzsche, Benjamin says, 'The fact that an author expresses himself in aphorisms will not count for anyone as proving anything against his systematic intentions.'[111] A syncretism of all thought that presents itself abstractly as a system of knowledge and 'weaves a spider's web between separate kinds of knowledge in an attempt to ensnare the truth,'[112] will inevitably fail to seize hold of it. In deciphering the content of truth in works of art, criticism must instead consider their relation, symbolic or otherwise, to the ideal of the problem, to the system, while carefully avoiding the temptation to identify it precisely. In fact, what the critic ultimately shows in the work of art

> is the virtual possibility of formulating the work's truth content as the highest philosophical problem. That before which it stops short, however—as if in awe of the work, but equally from

109 Benjamin, 'Goethe's *Elective Affinities*' in *SW*, VOL. 1, p. 334.

110 Benjamin, 'Goethe's *Elective Affinities*' in *SW*, VOL. 1, p. 334.

111 Benjamin, 'Concept of Criticism in German Romanticism' in *SW*, VOL. 1, p. 136.

112 Benjamin, *The Origin of German Tragic Drama*, p. 28.

> respect for the truth—is precisely this formulation itself. That possibility of formulation could indeed be realized only if the system could be the object of inquiry and thereby transform itself from an appearance of the ideal into the existence of the ideal—an existence that is never given. As such, however, it says simply that the truth in a work would be known not as something obtained in answer to a question, to be sure, but as something obtained on demand.[113]

In the same moment that it frees itself from the requirement of systematic construction, philosophy is compelled by its reflection on works of art to consider the thought of the system .

4. Beauty and truth

If the unity and totality of the solution of philosophical problems cannot be retraced, even if only symbolically, anywhere except in works of art, philosophy is destined to dissolve itself without residue in the allusivity of criticism, which thus becomes the only cognitive instrument adequate to deciphering beauty, whose virtual place resides in philosophy, since 'one may say that everything beautiful is connected in some way to the true.'[114] In any authentic work of art, we are dealing with a manifestation of the ideal of the problem.

> In the context of this consideration, criticism (where it is identical with interpretation and the opposite of all current methods of art appreciation) is the representation of an idea. Ideas' intensive infinitude characterizes them as monads. Allow me to define it: criticism is the mortification of works of art. Not that consciousness is enhanced in them (romantic!), but that knowledge takes up residence in them.[115]

---

113 Benjamin, 'Goethe's *Elective Affinities*' in *SW*, VOL. 1, p. 334.

114 Benjamin, 'Goethe's *Elective Affinities*' in *SW*, VOL. 1, p. 334.

115 Letter to Florens Christian Rang, 9 December 1923, in Benjamin, *Correspondence*, p. 224.

The preliminary clarification of the existing relation between truth and beauty is posited as a constitutional task of criticism, whose purpose is not to instruct or inform pedagogically, but rather, according to the 'Announcement of the Journal *Angelus Novus*', 'to cognize by immersing itself in the object', 'to concentrate on the individual work of art', and in so doing, 'to go beyond the results obtained by the Romantics.'[116] In this light, it will be above all necessary to seek to understand the meaning of the distinction Benjamin introduces with respect to the Romantic conception.

'An understanding of the Platonic view of the relationship of truth and beauty is not just a primary aim in every investigation into the philosophy of art, but it is indispensable to the definition of truth itself.'[117] The validity of the nexus between truth and beauty and the affirmation of the beautiful as the ontological predicate constitute definitive results for any speculation about art which does not want to fall into the empty pit of aestheticism and technicality. But nothing is decided about the value of that nexus, not even when the alternative is made as stark as possible. The crossroads is signalled by a sensitive critic whose friendship Benjamin cultivated:[118] 'Either beauty has nothing to do with truth, or beauty is truth', but the statement never provides any more exact indication on the nature of the path to be followed. Beauty, 'in some way relates to truth', but what is decisive is the interpretation of that way—if Nietzsche's intuition is correct that the points of rupture between the various philosophies are hidden in the subtlest shadings. In *Origin*, Benjamin illustrates truth as the 'essential content of beauty'. But the appropriation of this idea, which is canonical in Romantic speculative idealism from Schlegel to Hegel, becomes specified in Benjamin as he

116 Walter Benjamin, 'Announcement of the Journal *Angelus Novus*' in *SW*, VOL. 1, p. 293.

117 Benjamin, *The Origin of German Tragic Drama*, p. 30.

118 This is Charles Du Bos. The alternative is described in Charles Du Bos, *Che cos'è la letteratura*? (Florence: Libreria Grandangolo, 1949), p. 72 [Original edition: *What Is Literature*? (London: Sheed and Ward, 1940)]. The encounter between Benjamin and Du Bos is narrated by Werner Kraft, their intermediary, in 'Walter Benjamin hinter seinen Briefen', *Merkur* 21(3) (1967): 228.

clarifies how, through the work of art, this content introduces itself into beauty. And this depends ultimately on the way beauty arranges itself so as to receive it, and thus on what Benjamin holds to be beauty's philosophical content. This is synthetically declared in what is written on the front of a medallion (*Medaillon*) which makes a fine display of itself in the antique store (*Antiquitäten*) on the 'One-Way Street': 'In everything that is with reason called beautiful, appearance has a paradoxical effect.'[119] The guarantee that truth gives to the being of beauty depends, more radically, on the fact that the 'representational impulse in truth is the refuge of beauty as such.'[120] If in the work of art the duty of the critic is to show 'the virtual possibility of the formulation of its contents as a philosophical problem,'[121] this means that the latter does not reside immediately in the beautiful, but rather is mediated through appearances. The existence of truth is definitively identical with the appearance of the beautiful. But if this is so, criticism will never be able to assume a demythologizing process, as though beauty were the wrapping to be thrown away, beneath which truth shines in all its naked bluntness. 'In the face of everything beautiful, the idea of unveiling becomes that of the impossibility of unveiling. It is the idea of art criticism.'[122] Confronting the problem of interpreting the truth of individual artworks, criticism fulfils its task only when it recognizes that 'truth is not a process of exposure which destroys the secret, but a revelation which does justice to it.'[123] Truth as the content of beauty 'does not appear by being exposed', but rather, 'is revealed in a process which might be described metaphorically as the burning up of the husk as it enters the realm of ideas, that is to say a destruction of the work in which its external form achieves its most brilliant degree of illumination.'[124]

---

119 Benjamin, 'One-Way Street' in *SW*, VOL. 1, p. 466.

120 Benjamin, *Origin of German Tragic Drama*, p. 31.

121 Walter Benjamin, 'The Theory of Criticism' in *SW*, VOL. 1, p. 218.

122 Benjamin, 'Goethe's *Elective Affinities*' in *SW*, VOL. 1, p. 351.

123 Benjamin, *The Origin of German Tragic Drama*, p. 31.

124 Benjamin, *The Origin of German Tragic Drama*, p. 31.

The irreducibility of the nexus between truth and beauty needs to be justified by both poles. Otherwise, criticism would oscillate between the rigid manner of a demythologizing hermeneutics that annexes beauty to truth and the resigned attitude of an aestheticism that dissolves any truth-value. The apparently rational thesis that 'criticism is the mortification of works of art' here finds its occasion for an adequate evaluation. In addition to the cited letter to Rang, the idea appears also in *Origin*, where its anti-Romantic character is again stressed:

> Criticism is the mortification of the works [. . .] not then as the Romantics have it, awakening of the consciousness in living works, but the settlement of knowledge in dead ones . . . There is nothing of beauty which does not contain something that is worthy of knowledge. Philosophy must not attempt to deny that it re-awakens the beauty of works [. . .] Without at least an intuitive grasp of the life of the detail in the structure, all love of beauty is no more than empty dreaming.[125]

This calls for a recapitulation of the discussion of the system.

We have seen that the work of art is for Benjamin the only 'medium' that allows us to relate to the totality of philosophy. But this takes place on the condition of remaining aware that the system itself is configured in a dimension that is always essentially superior to what the set of all its problems would require. In effect, the unity of their solution can never be interrogated. It always remains a virtual demand that may be represented in works of art but can never find a solution. It may be true that among artworks the authentic ones have their siblings in the realm of philosophy and thus 'it is, after all, precisely these figures in which the ideal of philosophy's problem appears.'[126] But on the other hand, Benjamin always repeats that not even here can the formulability of the question concerning the system be resolved. Such formulability can never really become concrete, and the work subsists only as an apparition

---

125 Benjamin, *The Origin of German Tragic Drama*, p. 182.

126 Benjamin, 'Goethe's *Elective Affinities*' in *SW*, VOL. 1, p. 333.

of the ideal. It can never convert itself into the existence of the same ideal of which it is the secret utopia, despite alluding to it continuously. For this reason, works of art for Benjamin cannot be answers, but neither can they be questions. The truth within them cannot recognize itself as 'interrogated' (*erfragt*), but only as 'postulated and requested' (*erfordert*).[127] The character of making an appeal constantly inheres in the work of art, and it is the duty of the critic to provoke it and bring it to light in such a way as to produce in the reader an *Anstoss* [recoil].[128] Precisely because the work, to any authentic consideration, shows itself as infinitely provocative, the truth in beauty can only appear, but it can never claim to reunite itself once and for all with beauty in any sort of mystic unity. In this light, the Romantic exercise of hermeneutics appeared to Benjamin as invalidated, so to speak, by the vice of aestheticism. The 'fatal element' in Schlegel's pretence to grasp the system in an absolute manner configured itself in Benjamin's eyes as a transgression of the principle of the inexhaustibility of the meaning of the work of art. If the ideal of the problem—the system, the absolute—is able to become concrete once and for all, criticism will come to deprive itself of any value of originality. The artwork whose system realizes itself is, at the same time, consigned once and for all to the past, to tradition, to the museum. Criticism in such a vision is consequently nothing but inert contemplation.

Against the risk of this critical stasis, as presented in the aesthetic comportment of the Romantics, Benjamin set up a zone of tension between the sphere of commentary and that of criticism, aligning it with the dualism in every work of art between real content and truth content. This is also the zone of the discourse on criticism as the 'mortification of artworks', a genuine exponential elevation of the last among the thirteen theses in 'One-Way Street' that sustain the activity of the writer: 'The work is the death mask of its conception'[129] (this thesis varies

---

127 Benjamin, 'Goethe's *Elective Affinities*' in *SW*, VOL. 1, p. 334.

128 Benjamin, 'Goethe's *Elective Affinities*' in *SW*, VOL. 1, 333.

129 Benjamin, 'One-Way Street' in *SW*, VOL. 1, p. 459.

the formula contained in the letter to Florence Christian Rang of 10 January 1924: 'every perfect work is the death mask of its intuition.')[130]

> Critique seeks the truth content of a work of art; commentary, its material content. The relation between the two is determined by that basic law of literature according to which the more significant the work, the more inconspicuously and intimately its truth content is bound up with its material content.[131]

Along very similar lines, Benjamin writes in the *Origin*: 'The object of philosophical criticism is to show that the function of artistic form is as follows: to make historical content, such as provides the basis of every important work of art, into a philosophical truth.'[132] In the course of the history of the work, in fact, real content and truth content, initially entirely connected, separate from one another in the sense that the second comes to be hidden in the growing shadow projected over it by the real, inauthentic content.[133] This transfer of the effectual content into truth content carried out by criticism is expressed in an image in 'One-Way Street': 'Commentary and translation [a term interchangeable with "criticism" according to Novalis' conception, which Benjamin made his own][134] [. . .] on the tree of the sacred text [. . .] are only the eternally rustling leaves; on that of the profane, the seasonally falling fruits.'[135] The break between history and truth, in some way constitutive of action in the world, is removed only in God, such that an absolutely non-mythologizing reading can be performed only of the Bible. This break is paradigmatic instead in the exegesis of profane texts, forced to sew up the wound that constantly re-opens between real content and truth content. What's more, the search for the latter seems in effect impossible without

---

130 Benjamin, *Correspondence*, p. 227.

131 Benjamin, 'Goethe's *Elective Affinities*' in *SW*, VOL. 1, p. 297.

132 Benjamin, *The Origin of German Tragic Drama*, p. 182.

133 Benjamin, 'Goethe's *Elective Affinities*' in *SW*, VOL. 1, p. 297.

134 See Benjamin, 'Concept of Criticism in German Romanticism' in *SW*, VOL. 1, p. 154.

135 Benjamin, 'One-Way Street' in *SW*, VOL. 1, p. 449.

the requisite reward. In fact, 'the transubstantiation of material content into truth content' provokes 'a decay in effectiveness, whereby the original grace of an earlier charm diminishes decade by decade.' In exchange, however, this very process is 'the basis for a rebirth, in which all ephemeral beauty is completely stripped off, and the work stands as a ruin.'[136] The beautiful in fact can only subsist to the degree to which it is aware that only in the instant, in the moment of supreme fleetingness, can the truth achieve *existence*: 'It is questionable whether the beauty which endures does still deserve the name "ruin".'[137] This means that 'beauty remains brilliant and palpable as long as it freely admits to being so.'[138] Beauty knows that its refuge in truth is only and uniquely truth's representative moment. 'Its brilliance—seductive *as long as it wishes only to shine forth*—provokes pursuit by the intellect, and it reveals its innocence only by taking refuge on the altar of truth.'[139]

We have recognized the importance of not misunderstanding the fact that truth is beauty's content in the banal sense that beauty would therefore be nothing but illusory appearance, as though the truth of beauty could be revealed and uncovered. 'This formula—which, since truth is not in itself visible and its becoming visible could rest only on traits not its own, makes beauty into a semblance—amounts in the end, quite apart from its lack of method and reason, to philosophical barbarism.'[140] Truth appears in beauty only to the degree to which beauty is not a superfluous epiphenomenon. The meaning of Novalis' fable of the disciple in the temple of Sais who passionately seeks the mystery of nature, the veiled virgin, is decisive for Benjamin's conception. This disciple returns in the prologue to the *Origin* precisely as an admonishment that the person who tears away the final veil from the image of truth

---

136 Benjamin, *The Origin of German Tragic Drama*, p. 182 [translation modified].

137 Benjamin, *The Origin of German Tragic Drama*, p. 182.

138 Benjamin, *The Origin of German Tragic Drama*, p. 31.

139 Benjamin, *The Origin of German Tragic Drama*, p. 31 [italics added by the author].

140 Benjamin, 'Goethe's *Elective Affinities*' in *SW*, VOL. 1, p. 351.

will be destroyed by that vision.[141] (The appearance of beauty is not 'the superfluous veiling of things in themselves but rather the necessary veiling of things for us.')[142] The task of beauty is not to render visible the idea of truth, but its secret.

> Beauty is not a semblance, not a veil covering something else. It itself is not appearance but purely essence [. . .] For the beautiful is neither the veil nor the veiled object but rather the object in its veil [. . .] the task of art criticism is not to lift the veil but rather, through the most precise knowledge of it as a veil, to raise itself for the first time to the true view of the beautiful.[143]

Only when it comes to beauty is the paradox that essence is appearance valid. This can lead to a much broader discourse on the philosophy of history, founded on the division of the world into the opposed dimensions of mystery and revelation. 'That is to say, the same forces that become explosively and extensively temporal in the world of revelation (and this is what history is) appear concentrated in the silent [*Verschlossenheit*] world (and this is the world of nature and of works of art).'[144] In this phase of his thought, then, Benjamin holds that beauty can subsist only where, unlike in history, the separation between nudity and covering, the decipherment of the mystery, is not given: in art understood as a manifestation of nature. Only at the end of his dissertation, in his discussion of the category of the origin in light of Goethe's category of the typical, does he add further illumination to the connection made here between beauty and the natural object (to which pertains the work of art). But we should dwell here on the deductions that this nexus imposes on Benjamin.

---

141 See Benjamin, *The Origin of German Tragic Drama*, p. 36.

142 Benjamin, 'Goethe's *Elective Affinities*' in *SW*, VOL. 1, p. 351.

143 Benjamin, 'Goethe's *Elective Affinities*' in *SW*, VOL. 1, p. 351.

144 Letter to Florens Christian Rang, 9 December 1923, in Benjamin, *Correspondence*, p. 224.

'In veilless nakedness the essentially beautiful has withdrawn, and in the naked body of the human being is attained a being beyond all beauty—the sublime—and a work beyond all creations—that of the creator.'[145] There is implicit here a bitter polemic towards the adepts of the circle of Stefan George, whose conception of beauty Benjamin reviles as a crude and gross equivocation. Beauty, as we've seen, lives in the world of silence. Artworks are neither questions nor answers, which is why masterpieces are mute. Only in revelation lives the power of the name: 'The highest mental region of religion is (in the concept of revelation) at the same time the only one that does not know the inexpressible. For it is addressed in the name and expresses itself as revelation.'[146] Now ideas, towards which works of art always tend, however allusively, are (to return once again to the letter to Rang),

> the stars, in contrast to the sun of revelation. They do not shine their light into the day of history, but work within it invisibly. They shine their light only into the night of nature. Works of art are thus defined as models of a nature that does not await the day and thus does not await the judgement day either; they are defined as models of a nature that is neither the staging ground of history nor a human domicile.[147]

The sphere of creation which the George school considers the true space of the poet belongs instead, according to Benjamin, to the world of history and thus cannot know—given the unveiling of mystery inherent to this world—the meaning of the beauty whose divine foundation resides only in the secret. And, in reality, 'the artist is less the primal ground or creator than the origin or form-giver [*Bildner*], and certainly his work is not at any price his creature but rather his form [*Gebilde*].'[148]

---

145 Benjamin, 'Goethe's *Elective Affinities*' in *SW*, VOL. 1, p. 351.

146 Benjamin, 'On Language as Such and on the Language of Man' in *SW*, VOL. 1, p. 67.

147 Benjamin, *Correspondence*, p. 224.

148 Benjamin, 'Goethe's *Elective Affinities*' in *SW*, VOL. 1, pp. 323–24.

The concept of revelation (and that of creation which connects to it) do not know the inexpressible, as Benjamin had shown in his writing on language in 1916. 'The expression that is linguistically most existent (that is, most fixed) is linguistically the most rounded and definitive; in a word, the most expressed is at the same time the purely mental.'[149] But nature, the reverse of the spiritual, is 'mute'.[150] This is why in the work of art beauty paradoxically seems to express itself fully only in the degree to which it is stretched by the artist to the limit of what can be represented, to the point that it is devoid of expression (*das Ausdrucklose*).

> The expressionless is the critical violence which, while unable to separate semblance from essence in art, prevents them from mingling. It possesses this violence as a moral dictum. In the expressionless, the sublime violence of the true appears as that which determines the language of the real world according to the laws of the moral world.[151]

The model of this conception seems to be silence, the becoming mute of the tragic hero, which Benjamin theorized immediately after the writing on language in the essay on 'Fate and Character'. The results achieved on that occasion remained definitive for Benjamin, to the point that he transferred them whole into the *Origin*.[152] It is to the merit of Philippe Ivernel to have grasped in the *Origin*, even within the limits of a brief article, the specular significance of the two couples of concepts: revelation (power of the name)–tragedy (silence).[153] We may turn his penetrating observation to the issue at hand. We need only understand metonymically the couple tragedy (silence) as the relation between art (and, as we've

---

149 Benjamin, 'On Language as Such and on the Language of Man' in *SW*, VOL. 1, p. 67.

150 Benjamin, 'On Language as Such and on the Language of Man' in *SW*, VOL. 1, p. 72.

151 Benjamin, 'Goethe's *Elective Affinities*' in *SW*, VOL. 1, p. 340.

152 Benjamin, *The Origin of German Tragic Drama*, p. 108.

153 Philippe Ivernel, 'De la métaphysique du langage à la politique marxiste', *Le Monde* (31 May 1969).

seen, nature as well) and the *Ausdrucklose* (of which silence is simply one example).

The unexpressed for Benjamin is not the external technical artifice of a single artwork or artistic genre but a genuine category of language and art. Only such a concept is able to preserve art from the risk of falling into magical evocation, which is the characteristic assigned to it by any mythical and eroticizing conception of artistic production. The 'nocturnal character of the work' must be guaranteed; otherwise, if it were produced in a completely and openly unfolded manner, it would degenerate into a semblance, in the sense of being an empty construction, a veil whose veiling function is inessential. No light can be distinguished in the open sun, and the stars shine only against the dark background of the night sky. Whence Benjamin's opposition to the pretence of the concept of creation to summon the artwork forth from nothingness, ending up with nothing in your hands but a totality that is 'false, the mendacious, the aberrant—in short, the absolute.'[154] Creation is a mythical category. But then, returning to our point of departure—and recalling that creation, revelation and history position themselves in the same dimension—we would seem to derive the paradoxical conclusion that history has a family relation with myth. Benjamin's later encounter with the Marxian category of 'prehistory', matured through the development of the concept of *Naturgeschichte* in the *Origin*, here finds its truest prelude. For Benjamin, just as for Kafka, as Adorno pointed out, 'no progress has taken place at all.'[155] The same relation holds between art and myth as between myth and truth; that is, a relation of reciprocal exclusion.

> There is no truth, for there is no unequivocalness—and hence not even error—in myth [. . .] there is, as far as the spirit of myth is concerned, only a knowledge of it [. . .] Therefore, in Greece genuine art and genuine philosophy—as distinct from their inauthentic stage, the theurgic—begin with the departure of myth, because art is not based on truth to any lesser extent

154 Walter Benjamin, 'On Semblance' in *SW*, VOL. 1, p. 225.

155 Adorno, *Über Walter Benjamin*, p. 79.

> than is philosophy, and philosophy is not based on truth to any greater extent than is art.[156]

The construction of these two opposed but parallel series—myth–creation–knowledge on one side, nature–art–truth on the other—must now take account of the concept of beauty, which is here the point under discussion. Only the power of the unexpressed is able to guarantee the presence in beauty of the truth, because only the unexpressed guarantees the inexhaustibility of truth and banishes any pretence to reduce it to total knowledge in a semblance oblivious to its integral caducity. The truth cannot reach *existence* for more than an instant. Form (counterbalancing the magic formula of the mythical) also enchants chaos into the world, of course, but only—and this is crucial—'for an instant'.

> No work of art may appear completely alive without becoming mere semblance, and ceasing to be a work of art. The life quivering in it must appear petrified and as if spellbound in a single moment. The life quivering within it is beauty, the harmony that flows through chaos [. . .] What arrests this semblance, what holds life spellbound and disrupts the harmony, is the expressionless [*das Ausdruckslose*]. That quivering is what constitutes the beauty of the work; the paralysis is what defines its truth.[157]

The privileged sphere of artistic practice stands exclusively on the imperfection of the instruments used, such that the work lives only by virtue of the gaps that separate it from the hypothetical norm, in the same way a language understood to be an instrument perfectly adapted to render thought would suppress the poet, and would render communication impossible among people as well.

For truth to subsist in a work of art, there must be a continuing memory of the conflict particular to it between, on the one hand, the pretence of presenting itself as a world summoned forth out of nothing

---

156 Benjamin, 'Goethe's *Elective Affinities*' in *SW*, VOL. 1, p. 326.

157 Benjamin, 'On Semblance' in *SW*, VOL. 1, p. 224.

and concluded once and for all, and, on the other, the awareness of precariousness, of the 'instantaneity' of its happening. The 'mortification of artworks', which the critic must actualize, consists in nothing but guiding the pride of their beauty back to the humility that recognizes the source of that beauty in the

> caesura, in which, along with harmony, every expression simultaneously comes to a standstill, in order to give free reign to an expressionless power inside all artistic media. Such power has rarely become clearer than in Greek tragedy, on one hand, and in Hölderlin's hymnic poetry, on the other. Perceptible in tragedy as the falling silent of the hero, and in the hymn as an arrest in the rhythm. Indeed, one could not characterize this rhythm any more aptly than by asserting that something beyond the poet interrupts the language of the poetry.[158]

The authority of the unexpressed is a *moral* authority because it opposes the will to domination, the absolutizing pretence that beauty arouses in every 'auratic' conception of art (adopting here a term from the later Benjamin). Proof of this formulation is seen in the parallelism of the polemic *vis*: if in 'Goethe's *Elective Affinities*' the target is Friedrich Gundolf, in the work of 1936 on the technical reproducibility of the work of art, Benjamin aims his arrows against any 'cultic' conception of art, reminding us that a pagan exaltation of myth and ritual were constituent elements of the George school, with which Gundolf was affiliated. Against this, the 1934 essay on Kafka will provide a more felicitious demonstration of the moral law behind which beauty resides, held up by the forces of the unexpressed, which 'alone completes the work, by shattering it into a thing of shards, into a fragment of the true world, into the torso of a symbol.'[159]

'Rather, beauty appears in Kafka's world only in the most obscure places—among the accused persons, for example'. This is because there

---

158 Benjamin, 'Goethe's *Elective Affinities*' in *SW*, VOL. 1, p. 341 .

159 Benjamin, 'Goethe's *Elective Affinities*' in *SW*, VOL. 1, p. 340.

is something in the proceedings carried out against the accused that changes them. 'From *The Trial* it may be seen that these proceedings usually are hopeless for those accused—hopeless even when they have hopes of being acquitted. It may be this hopelessness that brings out the beauty in them—the only creatures in Kafka thus favoured.'[160] But the unreality of the desperation, the *ponderación misteriosa*, the intervention of God to recuperate the *disiecta membra* of the work of art had already been the unintended outlet of the long exploration of baroque drama. 'In the spirit of allegory it is conceived from the outset as a ruin, a fragment. Others may shine resplendently as on the first day; this form preserves the image of beauty to the very last.'[161] It is not, therefore that beauty simply substitutes hope like a banal echo of Stendhal's formula that beauty is a 'promise of happiness'. For Benjamin, only music can legitimately make this claim, because only to it does there belong 'a beauty that is no longer arrested by semblance.'[162] Goethe's last love in Marienbad found 'Reconciliation' in the domain of music in the third poem of the *Trilogy of Passion*.[163] Similarly with the brief streak of the falling star that Goethe evokes as an image of hope, that 'double delight from music and from love'[164] of the tormented lovers of the *Elective Affinities*, when the almost hopeless shimmer of dawn 'gleams [. . .] not at all as a fulfilment but rather as a first weak premonition.'[165] That beauty should take the place of hope cannot thus be Benjamin's last word on

---

160 Walter Benjamin, *Illuminations* (Hannah Arendt ed., Harry Zohn trans.) (New York: Schocken, 2007), pp. 115–16.

161 Benjamin, *The Origin of German Tragic Drama*, p. 235.

162 Benjamin, 'Goethe's *Elective Affinities*' in *SW*, VOL. 1, p. 348.

163 On the *Trilogy of Passion*, see Charles Du Bos, 'L'ultimo amore di Goethe e l'elegia di Marienbad' in Johann Wolfgang Goethe, *Trilogia della passione* (Giovanna Bemporad trans.) (Brescia: Morcelliana, 1952).

164 Johann Wolfgang von Goethe, 'Reconciliation (*Ein Gleichnis*)', from 'Trilogy of Passion (1823–1824)' (John Frederick Nims trans.), in *Collected Works, Volume I: Selected Poems* (Christopher Middleton ed.) (Princeton, NJ: Princeton University Press, 1994), p. 255.

165 Benjamin, 'Goethe's *Elective Affinities*' in *SW*, VOL. 1, p. 348.

the subject. 'Like a trembling question', at the end of the *Elective Affinities*, 'that "how beautiful" resounds in the ears of the dead' who, 'we hope, awaken, if ever, not to a beautiful world but to a blessed one.'[166] Only in this way can the final sentence of Goethe's novel, alluding to a gentle, future reawakening of the beloved couple from their mortal sleep, claim to be something more than a 'conciliatory flourish', as Thomas Mann justly branded it.[167]

While no artwork with a message will ever be able to communicate the essence of hope, neither can that essence radiate out from the semblance of conciliation that is offered by the beauty of a coldly executed artwork.

5. Art, nature and history

We have seen how Benjamin refused supinely to accept the Romantic conception of criticism—which he nevertheless considered important—and how he modified it in the sense of a progressive liberation from the ambiguous aesthetic mysticism of a figure such as Schlegel. We may now add that in the final chapter of his dissertation, Benjamin had provided a means to inoculate himself against the risks inherent in the Romantic attitude by proposing Goethe as a parallel and alternative to Schlegel.

This is the place to take up Benjamin's brief *excursus* on 'The Early Romantic Theory of Art and Goethe'.[168]

The Romantics had identified the essence of art in the determination of its idea. With the category of 'idea' they meant the 'a priori of a method,'[169] but they were completely uninterested in searching for an a

---

166 Benjamin, 'Goethe's *Elective Affinities*' in *SW*, VOL. 1, p. 355.

167 Thomas Mann, Introduction to Johann Wolfgang von Goethe, *The Permanent Goethe* (Thomas Mann ed.) (New York: The Dial Press, 1948), p. *xxxv*.

168 Benjamin, 'Concept of Criticism in German Romanticism' in *SW*, VOL. 1, p. 178–85. [See the translator's note on p. 199n307: 'The concluding section of Benjamin's dissertation was not submitted to the faculty; it was intended as an "esoteric afterword" for his friends and for the further development of his own thoughts.']

169 Benjamin, 'Concept of Criticism in German Romanticism' in *SW*, VOL. 1, p. 179.

priori of content to associate with that of method in any given work of art. In other words, Romantic formalism recognizes no 'ideal of art'. The point of departure of Goethe's philosophy of art is, instead, the attempt to grasp the a priori of content, since the question around which it orients itself is that of the ideal of art. The unity of this ideal is not of a medial type because it is manifested, on the contrary, 'in a limited, harmonic *discontinuum* of pure contents.'[170] Goethe's classicism envisioned the immediate antecedent of his doctrine in the Greek idea of the nine Muses subject to the sovereignty of Apollo. 'Just as, in contrast to the idea, the inner structure of the ideal is discontinuous, so, too, the connection of this ideal with art is not given in a medium but is designated by a refraction.'[171] Goethe defines these pure contents, which transcend the individual artwork, as archetypes (*die Urbilder*), and maintains that, although invisible, they may be grasped through intuition. Further, the Greeks are those who came closest to intuiting these contents, and that is why their works must become models for us (*Vorbildern*), second-degree archetypes. But the crucial element for Benjamin is the fact that for Goethe, art never creates its own archetypes, because 'they rest, prior to all created work, in that sphere of art where art is not creation but nature.'[172] It is to this sphere that Goethe refers with his theory of originary phenomena (*Urphänomene*) whose point of departure was the theory of the *Urpflanze*, conceived in Palermo during his trip to Italy in 1787. Goethe strove to ascertain the *Urphänomene* with the aim of grasping the idea of nature, so as to present the latter as an archetype of art, pure content. Nature, that is, replaces the Muses but the chance character of the relation between the individual artwork and the ideal of art does not change. 'In relation to the ideal, the single work remains, as it were, a torso. It is an individuated endeavour to represent the archetype.'[173] Nothing contrasted with Romantic intentions so strongly as Goethe's refusal to attempt the immediate conciliation of the conditional with

---

170 Benjamin, 'Concept of Criticism in German Romanticism' in *SW*, VOL. 1, p. 179.

171 Benjamin, 'Concept of Criticism in German Romanticism' in *SW*, VOL. 1, p. 179.

172 Benjamin, 'Concept of Criticism in German Romanticism' in *SW*, VOL. 1, p. 180.

173 Benjamin, 'Concept of Criticism in German Romanticism' in *SW*, VOL. 1, p. 181.

the unconditional. Much attention has been devoted to Friedrich Schlegel's plan to encompass the system in an absolute manner: the concept of form he elaborated is precisely based on overcoming any moment of chance, any attitude that would treat the artwork as contingent, as a torso.

> The Romantics define the relation of artworks to art as infinity in totality—which means that the infinity of art is fulfilled in the totality of works. Goethe defines it as unity in plurality—which means that the unity of art is found again and again in the plurality of works. This infinity is that of pure form; this unity is that of pure content [. . .] The idea of art is the idea of its form, as its ideal is the ideal of its content. Hence, the fundamental systematic question of the philosophy of art can be formulated as the question of the relation between the idea and the ideal of art.[174]

In this regard, the only possible solution for Benjamin seemed to consist in bringing into collision the opposed exigencies of the two positions. For while the Romantics had not been capable of grasping the idea of art, Goethe's concept of the archetype was not adequate to furnishing a solution to the problem of form. 'The intention that disclosed to him the depths of the problem of content in art became the source of a sublime naturalism in the face of the problem of form.'[175]

Benjamin interprets the categories elaborated in Goethe's philosophy of nature in an aesthetic sense. This was perfectly legitimate, because in doing so he knew that he was operating in concordance with Goethe himself:

> The place occupied in Goethe's writings by his scientific studies is the one which in lesser artists is commonly reserved for aesthetics [. . .] Goethe belongs to the family of great minds for whom there is basically no such thing as an art separated from

174 Benjamin, 'Concept of Criticism in German Romanticism' in *SW*, VOL. 1, p. 183.

175 Benjamin, 'Concept of Criticism in German Romanticism' in *SW*, VOL. 1, p. 184.

> life. In his eyes, the theory of the 'primal phenomenon' in science was also a theory of art, just as scholastic philosophy had been for Dante and the technical arts for Dürer.[176]

The tension that Goethean theory leaves unresolved, and upon which Benjamin will never tire of meditating, is that inherent in the identification of *Urbild* and *Ürphanomenon*. The dissertation had already recognized the aporias. These come down to the fact that such an identification overturns the previous thesis, according to which—in contrast to the Romantic idea—the ideal, the appearance of the absolute, the connection of pure contents can never offer itself up in a 'medium', but is always characterized by discontinuity. In effect, if the idea of nature that constitutes itself as pure content of art can be intuited in originary phenomena, what fades away is precisely that element of rupture which seemed inherent in the work of art, leaving interpretation to fall back hopelessly into a theory of mirroring. Not by chance, the archetype becomes a model. Behind this we find a fundamental ambiguity in the Goethean concept of nature, which Benjamin brings to light in his essay on 'Goethe's *Elective Affinities*'. Only here, at the same time, can Goethe's sovereign disinterest for the conception of the criticism of art be accounted for; that is why, in the dissertation, it remained more hinted at than explicated. The knowledge of nature was for Goethe the only standard by which artworks could be verified. They have no use for criticism. The fact remains, however, that this concept of nature equivocally

> designates in Goethe at once the sphere of perceptible phenomena and that of intuitable archetypes. At no time, however, was Goethe able to give an account of this synthesis [. . .] Since he did not define 'true' nature conceptually, he never penetrated to the fruitful centre of an intuition that bade him seek the presence of 'true' nature as *Ürphenomenon* in its appearances—something he presupposed in works of art.[177]

---

176 Walter Benjamin, 'Goethe' in *SW*, VOL. 2, PART 1: 1927–1930, pp. 179–80.

177 Benjamin, 'Goethe's *Elective Affinities*' in *SW*, VOL. 1, p. 314 .

A chaotic element thus attaches itself to this concept of nature, whose confines are never traced out, even as it expands gigantically to monstrous proportions. The world of originary phenomena, far from being clarified, collapses into a chaos of symbols. On the basis of this confused mixture of the two spheres that define nature, 'the *Ürphenomenon* as archetype [*Urbild*] too often turned into nature as model [*Vorbild*].'[178] In this sense, as the dissertation noted, the problem is not that of reducing the concept of nature totally within art, but of seeing how it appears to science. The misunderstanding in Goethe's conception can be resolved clearly once it is grasped that 'only in the domain of art do the Ür-phenomena—as ideals—present themselves adequately to perception, whereas in science they are replaced by the idea, which is capable of illuminating the object of perception but never of transforming it into an object of intuition.'[179]

For Benjamin, this idolatry of nature, with the consequent rejection of any criticism, configures the pagan aspect of Goethe's doctrine, because the effort to realize concretely the originary phenomena of nature, with no role for artistic intuition, is mythical. The failure to distinguish in nature the sphere that properly pertains to art, the confusion of archetype with originary phenomena, leads first of all to a banal conception of art as imitation, while it also betrays the otherwise correct exigencies contained in the concept of the *Ürphanomenon*.

Benjamin's encounter with the theory of the originary phenomenon also offers a decisive outlet for the conceptual difficulty that his text on the 'Program' had tackled with reference to Kantian philosophy. The Kantian alternatives were an abyss across which Goethe had thrown more than one footbridge, and the doctrine of the originary phenomenon aimed to eliminate the fracture between phenomenon and noumenon, individuating in the natural moment the supernatural that secretly directed it. But this function of mediation between phenomenon and idea belongs to the originary phenomenon, Benjamin argues, only in the degree to which it can be purified of the above-described mythological residue.

---

178 Benjamin, 'Goethe's *Elective Affinities*' in *SW*, vol. 1, p. 315.

179 Benjamin, 'Goethe's *Elective Affinities*' in *SW*, vol. 1, p. 315.

Benjamin alters the function of the originary phenomenon, transforming it, in the introduction to his *Origin*, from a category of nature into the historical concept of origin. This change in sign effected by Benjamin on the body of the Goethean concept does not aim at surpassing Goethe, but rather at bringing into focus the originary phenomenon's authentic characteristics (removing the mythical, which in Goethe always threatens to intrude). The passage of this concept *tout court* into the realm of history is possible specifically because, for Benjamin, human history has always had the petrified visage of nature. The Goethean derivation of the notion of origin cannot be drawn directly from the book on the *Trauerspiel* because the author never makes reference to it. Particularly revealing is this note from the manuscript 'Nachträge zum Trauerspielbuch' (Additions to the book on *Trauerspiel*):

> In studying Simmel's discussion of the Goethean concept of truth, particularly his excellent explanation of the concept of *Urphänomenon* [. . .] it became irrefutably clear to me that my concept of 'origin' in the book on the *Trauerspiel* is a rigorous and apt translation of this fundamental Goethean idea from the realm of nature to that of history. 'Origin'—this is the concept of the *Urphänomenon* theologically and historically different, theologically and historically living, and recuperated from the pagan nexus of nature to the Judaic nexus of history. '*Ursprung*'—this is *Urphänomenon* in a theological sense.[180]

The comprehension of the concept of 'origin' is central to any effort to comprehend the peculiarity of the study of baroque drama. The treatment in the book on the baroque is decisive not so much because the 'origin' is discussed as a philosophical concept in the 'Epistemo-Critical Prologue', but above all because the entire work (as announced in the title itself) is an incarnation of the problem, particularly in the two paradigmatic illustrations of the origin of the tragic from myth and the origin of the *Trauerspiel* from the baroque vision of history. Far from being a mere

---

180 Walter Benjamin, 'Nachträge zum Trauerspielbuch' in *Gesammelte Schriften*, VOL. 1, TOME 3, pp. 953–54.

epistemological category pre-existent to the investigation, the concept of the *Ursprung* came to be forged in the same terms as the ideas that find their expression in it. The traits studied in the object under examination reverberate upon the instrument used to examine them. The transfer of the Goethean concept of originary phenomenon into the order of history is possible only if history is seen as natural history, but this latter is also exactly the mark of the baroque vision of the world, which is the subject of the analysis. A genuine circle thus links the object and the method of research, in keeping with this thought's most authentic intention. The same, in fact, can be said, as we shall see, for the examination of allegory and for the technique of the montage of citations in the work on the Parisian *Passages*.[181]

Here we need to clarify why the *Ursprung* can work as a method only if history is understood in that particular 'anti-historicist' sense. The comparison with the Goethean *Urphänomenon* can serve as a foothold. Goethe's attention focused on the originary plant that stands behinds all plants. In the same way, the Benjaminian phenomenon of the origin identifies 'the form in which an idea will constantly confront the historical world, until it is revealed fulfilled, in the totality of its history.'[182] The concept of the life and survival of artworks is not, for Benjamin, a metaphorical concept, as though life were an attribute only of organic physicality. The discussion of beauty in 'Goethe's *Elective Affinities*' had already removed life from the stage of the theatre of nature, by negating, as we've seen, that beauty can inhere in the naked body of man. More explicitly, in the preface to the translation of Baudelaire's *Tableaux Parisiens*, we find the claim that

> the concept of life is given its due only if everything that has a history of its own, and is not merely the setting for history, is credited with life. In the final analysis, the range of life must be

---

181 Renato Solmi has grasped this extremely well in his introduction to the translations collected in Walter Benjamin, *Angelus Novus* (Renato Solmi trans.) (Turin: Einaudi, 1962), p. *xv*.

182 Benjamin, *Origin of German Tragic Drama*, pp. 45–46.

> determined by the standpoint of history rather than that of nature.[183]

For Benjamin, 'dialectics at a standstill' must apply to history just as it does to nature. In fact, what escapes the causal dialectic triggered by the mechanism of determinate negation is a notion basic to the comprehension of Goethe's originary phenomenon; that is, the concept of entelechy. The first draft of the prologue to the book on the baroque affirmed this explicitly: 'So the origin is entelechy. In entelechy, becoming presents itself [*Ursprung also ist Entelechie. In der Entelechie stellt das Werden sich*].'[184] But the principle is no less clear in the paragraph on monadology in the definitive version of the book, where the concept of natural history is again mentioned explicitly:

> that which is comprehended in the idea of origin still has history, in the sense of content, but not in the sense of a set of occurrences which have befallen it. Its history is inward in character and is not to be understood as something boundless, but as something related to essential being, and it can therefore be described as the past and subsequent history of this being. The past and the subsequent history of such essences is—as a token of their having been redeemed or gathered into the world of ideas—not pure history, but natural history.[185]

But the life of forms is per excellence a natural life and, for this reason, Goethe's bequest of the notion of originary phenomenon can be profitably applied particularly in the discussion of the cataloguing of forms, in the realm of what are traditionally called literary genres.

The refusal to admit any possible genre between the universal of art and the particular of the individual artwork has its root in the confusion between concept and idea. Goethe's *Urphänomenon* was anything but an abstract classification: its function was exquisitely medial.

---

183 Walter Benjamin, 'The Task of the Translator' in *SW*, VOL. 1, p. 255.

184 Benjamin, *Gesammelte Schriften*, VOL. 1, TOME 3, p. 946.

185 Benjamin, *The Origin of German Tragic Drama*, p. 47.

> There prevails in his writings a relationship of the 'particular' to the 'universal' such as can hardly be found elsewhere in the history of philosophy or of natural science. It was his firm conviction that the particular and the universal are not only intimately connected but that they interpenetrate one another.[186]

For Benjamin, the *Urphänomenon* presents itself as the only epistemological canon capable of avoiding the brutal liquidation of the particular and, at the same time, the syllogistic nexus of empiricity devoid of leaps and ruptures. That is the discontinuity which the dissertation had instead identified in the relation between Goethe's 'pure contents' of art and art's concrete formations. Aesthetic ideas are not abstract classifications that aim to annex a group of artworks after having disrobed them of any eccentricity in their dress and reduced them to pragmatic uniformity. The same goes for the concept of knowledge. But the category of origin is not a logical category. The brief note in this sense alluding to Cohen in the *Origin*[187] had been more substantially presented in an early work, published posthumously, on 'Language and Logic'. There it was explained that,

> the question of origins is quite different from the pseudo-question of origins in the relations between concept and sub-concept. For here the derivation is an illusion, since the mode and number of specifics of the concept that occur in the sub-concept are a matter of chance. In contrast, every essence possesses from the outset a limited—and moreover determinate—multiplicity of essences, which do not derive from the unity in a deductive sense but are empirically assigned to it as the condition of its representation and articulation. The essential unity reigns

186 Ernst Cassirer, 'The Idea of Metamorphosis and Idealistic Morphology: Goethe' in *The Problem of Knowledge: Philosophy, Science and History since Hegel* (William H. Woglom and Charles W. Hendel trans) (New Haven, CT: Yale University Press, 1950), p. 145.

187 See Benjamin, *The Origin of German Tragic Drama*, pp. 45–46.

> over a multiplicity of essences in which it manifests itself, but from which it always remains distinct.[188]

Just as for Goethe, for Benjamin too, the relation between the general and the particular 'is not one of logical subsumption but of ideal or "symbolic" representation.'[189]

Benjamin here found himself facing one of the most characteristic either/or's in the history of logic, that which is commonly presented as the alternative of genesis versus validity. In this regard, his polemic against the positions expressed by a representative of 'pure' history such as Croce is important. The force of his objections to the dissolution of genres theorized by Croce is entirely bent on confronting the apparent attenuation of Croce's own doctrine as proposed in this passage: 'When we denied theoretic value to abstract classifications, we did not intend to deny it to that genetic and concrete classification which is not, indeed, a "classification" and is called History.'[190] In Crocean historicism, as Benjamin sees it, the apparent recognition of the particular is only the pretext for a more subtle 'will to power' of the universal. In Crocean doctrine, no screen protects the historical element from the overweening domination of the all-encompassing. 'Considered philosophically, nothing is interspersed between the universal and the individual, no sequence of genres or species, no *generalia*.'[191] But this impure mixture—where nothing recognizes the autonomy of the historical and nothing 'rescues' it from sinking in the turbid waves of the uncontrollable river of dialectic—is mythological. The flipside of absolutist idealism is empiricism in the observation of phenomena. What escapes it, according to Benjamin, is the particular form of 'idea' that the artistic genre assumes once it is configured as an originary phenomenon.

---

188 Walter Benjamin, 'Language and Logic (I–III)' in *SW*, VOL. 1, p. 273.

189 Cassirer, 'Idea of Metamorphosis and Idealistic Morphology: Goethe', p. 146.

190 Benedetto Croce, *The Essence of Aesthetic* (Douglas Ainslie trans.) (London: Heinemann, 1921), p. 59; cited in Benjamin, *Origin of German Tragic Drama*, p. 45.

191 Croce, *Essence of Aesthetic*, p. 57; cited in Benjamin, *Origin of German Tragic Drama*, pp. 43–44: 'No intermediate element interposes itself philosophically between the universal and the particular, no series of kinds or species, or generalia.'

The world of phenomena—which in the realm of aesthetics is the history of artworks—is not suppressed by the unity of essence that supports it, because the origin is not delineated as an 'entity' but as a force field, a tensional space inside which the individual phenomenon becomes totality and loses any episodic character. The historical element which thus belongs to the origin cannot be absolutized, cannot be understood as an overturning of rigid abstraction, as a genesis in the mode of Croce. 'Origin [*Ursprung*], although an entirely historical category, has, nevertheless, nothing to do with genesis [*Enstehung*]. The term origin is not intended to describe the process by which the existent came into being, but rather to describe that which emerges from the process of becoming and disappearance.'[192] The origin is not the beginning in the familiar sense of the term. It never reveals itself to the gaze fixed on the mere given fact, on the phenomenon considered in its presence.

> That which is original is never revealed in the naked and manifest existence of the factual; its rhythm is apparent only to a dual insight. On the one hand it needs to be recognized as a process of restoration and reestablishment, but on the other hand, and precisely because of this, as something imperfect and incomplete.[193]

The refusal to attribute a sort of 'presentness' to the originary signifies that the value of phenomena can never come simply from their juxtaposition in an uninterrupted sequence, offering itself up to be registered by a historicist methodology. No light of novelty will ever come effulgently to shatter this world, where artworks pile up to the point of impeding, in their unrecognizability, any possibility of dialogue or encounter. Benjamin's concept of origin is inseparably connected to the notion of discontinuity, the awareness that the idea of a form of art is not a label in a catalogue, because the artworks included there open historical constellations of truth.

---

192 Benjamin, *Origin of German Tragic Drama*, p. 45.

193 Benjamin, *The Origin of German Tragic Drama*, p. 45.

> Origin is an eddy in the stream of becoming, and in its current it swallows the material involved in the process of genesis. That which is original is never revealed in the naked and manifest existence of the factual [. . .] There takes place in every original phenomenon a determination of the form in which an idea will constantly confront the historical world, until it is revealed fulfilled, in the totality of its history.[194]

But what philosophical approach is adequate to grasping the phenomenon of origin in the endless panorama of works of art? Wouldn't the absence of any criterion lead to an indiscriminate arbitrariness in the choice? Here gapes again the abyss of mythology that Benjamin had reproached in the limitless dispersion of originary phenomena in Goethe's philosophy of nature. But, as Benjamin sees it, philosophical meditation can find the reasons it needs to obey on condition it returns to the dialectic that moves the concept of origin, characterized by a singular interweaving of uniqueness and repetition. Although Benjamin makes the claim only indirectly, these are the signs of 'authenticity', because only with reference to the authentic does what Benjamin juxtaposed as a program to Max Kommerell's *Der Dichter als Führer in der Deutschen Klassik* (The Poet as Leader in German Classicism), possess validity. 'We must declare our preference for the unvarnished truth, for a laconic conception of the seminal, of fertility; and this means opting for the realm of theory and bidding farewell to the world of "vision" [*Schau*].'[195] The authentic is unique but would no longer be so if this uniqueness configured itself as the sterility of the exceptional, the unrepeatable, as an infertile 'point of view' withdrawn from the innumerable initiatives that go under the heading of theory. The Hegelian 'so much the worse for facts' is for Benjamin the axiom of a cognitive hauteur that will never be able to

---

194 Benjamin, *The Origin of German Tragic Drama*, pp. 45–46. [This citation in the English translation is quite different in tone and possibly substance from Carchia's Italian. In Carchia, it is not an 'eddy' but a *vortice*, not a 'stream' but a *fiume*, not a 'process of genesis' but a *nascita*. —Trans.]

195 Walter Benjamin, 'Against a Masterpiece' in *SW*, VOL. 2, PART 1, p. 383.

encounter the inexhaustible seed of truth hidden in the phenomenon of origin. 'Because every proof of origin must be prepared to face up to the question of its authenticity.'[196] It is not, therefore, a matter of seizing in the origin an atemporal truth, an eternal principle at the base of history. The mark of repetition is the only thing that saves truth from the pretence, inspired by maniacal purity, to be already and forever deployed against, and refractory to, any mundane contamination.

Here Benjamin has already made his own Karl Kraus's formula 'Origin is the goal', which he would always observe scrupulously, to the point of making it the motto of the fourteenth thesis of his 'On the Concept of History'.[197] In his 1934 essay on the Austrian writer, where this formula appears for the first time, Benjamin notes that 'this "origin"—the seal of authenticity on the phenomenon—is the subject of a discovery that has a curious element of recognition.'[198] This statement is taken in its entirety, without citation (a practice dear to Benjamin), from the *Origin*, with a slight but highly significant variation that consists in the inversion in the position of the two concepts, 'origin' and 'authentic'. In the *Origin*, the beginning of the sentence goes, 'The authentic—that hallmark of origin in phenomena [. . .]'[199] The notion of 'discovery' in the first draft of the book on the baroque was still theologically bound to the idea of revelation:

> Everything that is origin appears only as a doubly determined being: everything that is origin is an incomplete restoration of Revelation. If it were complete, it would be more than origin or element, namely, thing and more than part of the idea; that is, truth. If it were not reflected in revelation, there would be no sign of its originality.[200]

---

196 Benjamin, *The Origin of German Tragic Drama*, p. 46.

197 Benjamin, 'On the Concept of History' in *SW*, VOL. 4, p. 395.

198 Walter Benjamin, 'Karl Kraus' in *SW*, VOL. 2, PART 2: 1931–1934, p. 451.

199 Benjamin, *The Origin of German Tragic Drama*, p. 46.

200 First draft of the Introduction to the *Origin of German Tragic Drama*; Benjamin, *Gesammelte Schriften*, VOL. 1, TOME 3, p. 935.

But the characteristic inconclusiveness of the authentic (and, indifferently, of the origin) came subsequently to be more and more precisely delineated through a series of still-imprecise terms such as 'restoration', 'renovation', 'repetition', and finally the definitive inconclusiveness of 'recognize' (*Wiedererkennen*). It is not for nothing that this is the primary obstacle for any philosophy that posits itself as a deductive nexus devoid of residue and totally resolved. And yet, furnishing proof of origin by probing the authenticity of what is observed 'would seem to do away with the distinction between the *quaestio juris* and the *quaestio facti* as far as the highest objects of philosophy are concerned.'[201] This, Benjamin observes, is 'indisputable and inevitable'.[202] Opposition to this separation had been the particular impulse of his philosophy, as the text on the 'Program' makes plain. But as to the truth of the origin, which of its fecund consequences offers itself to the permanent openness of this recognition? Here, Benjamin implies, the element of unicity, the dimension of 'idea' that pertains to the authenticity of origin, must protect against the dissolving pretences of anyone who claims that any *frühe "Faktum"* (previous fact) in itself attains to essence.[203] The 'recognition' that the philosopher elaborates is never blind, but always internally motivated by the light of the idea. 'Indeed this is where the task of the investigator begins, for he cannot regard such a fact as certain until its innermost structure appears to be so essential as to reveal it as an origin.'[204] No guide or method can claim any higher certainty than that which is inspired by truth itself.

A more precise articulation of philosophical research as to originary phenomena leads to the determination that it 'is the form which, in the remotest extremes and the apparent excesses of the process of development, reveals the configuration of the idea—the sum total of all possible

201 Benjamin, *The Origin of German Tragic Drama*, p. 46.

202 Benjamin, *The Origin of German Tragic Drama*, p. 46.

203 Benjamin, *The Origin of German Tragic Drama*, p. 46.

204 Benjamin, *The Origin of German Tragic Drama*, p. 46.

meaningful juxtapositions of such opposites.'[205] The parallelism with Goethe's *Urphänomenon* here finds another verification in the category of the extreme. It is probable, in fact, that it is a re-elaboration, in the realm of history, of the notion of polarity that pertains to Goethe's philosophy of nature. The polar relation between the individual parts and between these and the whole is the hallmark of organicity in Goethe's construction. Latent in the isolated natural phenomenon is a drive towards totality, just as it is only thanks to the whole that this tension can manifest itself. The whole of nature seems to constitute itself, in Goethe, as that constitutive idea of nature whose possibility was negated by the Kantian 'critique of theological judgement'. But it is less risky to attribute such a character of the constituent idea in a Kantian sense to the relation of origin studied in the *Ursprung*. In Benjamin, there is no totality of artworks to which the individual exemplars relate in an inseparable nexus like parts within a whole. The notion of totality is not ever, so to speak, 'entity-ized', and the dialectic of unicity and repetition of the origin is not that between a principle of individuation and an opposed one that negates it, incorporating it into a conclusive totality. The notion of the extreme (*Extrem*), on the other hand, does not submit easily to 'dialectization'.

> In literary-historical analysis, differences and extremes are bought together in order that they might be relativized in evolutionary terms; in a conceptual treatment they acquire the status of complementary forces, and history is seen as no more than the coloured border to their crystalline simultaneity.[206]

The virtuality of history's unfolding course impedes the dialectic of extremes from fixing itself around the moment of synthesis. The extremes do not relate to one another reciprocally and antithetically, as though such reciprocal clashing would trigger the superior moment of totality. This is, in fact, precisely the function of history in any dialectic whose

---

205 Benjamin, *The Origin of German Tragic Drama*, p. 47.

206 Benjamin, *The Origin of German Tragic Drama*, p. 38.

propulsive centre is the concept of determinate negation. But the truth, which in Benjamin shoots out like sparks from the clash of the extremes, does not remove their opposition; it does not smooth out their sharp points, reining them together within the levelling flow of history. 'The idea is the extreme example of a form or genre, and as such does not enter into the history of literature.'[207] Only to the extent that it is not an amorphous totality, in which emergent uniformities coincide to dissolve in a historicist panorama, can the moment of synthesis, the point of equilibrium, become fertile for ulterior openings. In the virtual course of history, the unity of the idea opens to reveal ever new extreme valences. One could describe Benjamin's procedure here as the most paradoxical reversal of the Hegelian dialectic. In Hegel, the millstone of history turns, in its perpetual motion, for no other reason than to come to stasis in the final synthesis. But in Benjamin it's just the opposite. The interpretative infinity of the idea can oppose the dead stasis of the concept only because the historical process becomes immobilized, the becoming of the phenomenon freezes in the moment of the idea.

> The tendency of all philosophical conceptualization is thus redefined in the old sense: to establish the becoming of phenomena in their being. For in the science of philosophy the concept of being is not satisfied by the phenomenon until it has absorbed all its history. In such investigations this historical perspective can be extended, into the past or the future, without being subject to any limits of principle. This gives the idea its total scope. And its structure is a monadological one, imposed by totality in contrast to its own inalienable isolation.[208]

If the idea must stand as a force field, it cannot reduce itself to its constituent elements, and that image must be understood not in a metaphorical sense, but as a real space. An actual short circuit seems to take place here between this methodological necessity and the treatment of the

---

207 Benjamin, *The Origin of German Tragic Drama*, p. 38.

208 Benjamin, *The Origin of German Tragic Drama*, p. 47.

baroque concept of the world. The integral secularization in this concept, which takes place within the historicity of the creatural state, the shifting of history into the theatre of action, expresses 'the same metaphysical tendency which simultaneously led, in the exact sciences, to the infinitesimal method. In both cases chronological movement is grasped and analysed in a spatial image.'[209] The parallel between Leibniz and the baroque *Weltanschauung* balances perfectly in the methodological vision of the idea as monad.

It is a matter therefore of seeing the content of truth, which for Benjamin is concealed in the representation of the idea as monad, beyond the manner in which Leibniz receives the term, and still further, beyond that of the doctrine of idea-numbers in the late Plato's speculations.[210]

The definition of the idea as monad presented itself quite naturally to Benjamin as the only one able to respond to the peculiar characteristics of his philosophical method. In its central intention, in fact, the dialectic of the authentic led directly away from the antithesis between the eternal element and the historical one, and freed Benjamin from the necessity of constructing the latter as an interchangeable detail in the sovereign unfolding of the world spirit. Because it renders virtual the course of the particular, the link between unicity and repetition that pertains to the phenomenon of origin saves the particular's most legitimate requirements. History, understood as a 'coloured border' of the idea that flashes between extremes, thus avoids reduction to a tautological exemplification of a pre-existent spiritual absolute that is bound to incorporate it. In Benjamin, the Eleatic immobilization of temporal flux and the philosophy of the infinitesimal aim to shatter the prejudice that attributes to totality predominance over phenomena, precisely when that prejudice recognizes that totality is grounded on the necessary concatenation of phenomena,

---

209 Benjamin, *The Origin of German Tragic Drama*, p. 92.

210 Benjamin alludes to the equalization of ideas with numbers in his important letter dated 9 December 1923 (*Correspondence*, p. 224) to Rang: '[F]or Leibniz, the discontinuity of whole numbers was a phenomenon crucial for his theory of monads.' An explicit reference to Plato's *Timaeus* follows.

that is, at the price of their insignificance. This intuition is expressed in the most convincing manner in the characteristic affirmation according to which, 'the smallest cell of visualized reality outweighs the rest of the world '.[211] The suspension of historical movement into a static nucleus subject to the most intense observation thus configures the monadological process. But with this, the process sediments itself into image. The theory of the dialectical image, which begins its elaboration starting from the aphorisms of 'One-Way Street', did not arise out of nothing. The encounter with the Surrealist 'fulgurations', the technique of the 'snapshots', of the montage of citations, are merely the prolongation of a philosophical *intentio* made explicit in its results from the very beginning. It is already fully present in the definition of philosophical representation as *Umweg* (detour). If in such a representation the object must be taken as the pretext for a reservoir of allusions that is in principle infinite, this is possible only on condition of knowing how to practice what Benjamin calls, 'the interpolation into the extremely small'—to borrow the expression used in the illustration that accompanies the shopwindow of the 'Fan' in 'One-Way Street'.

> The faculty of imagination is the gift of interpolating into the infinitely small, of inventing, for every intensity, an extensiveness to contain its new, compressed fullness,[212] in short, receiving each image as if it were that of the folded fan, which only in spreading draws breath and flourishes, in its new expanse, the beloved features within it.[213]

---

211 Adorno cited these words of Benjamin in various writings; see, for example, Theodor W. Adorno, *Negative Dialectics* (E. B. Ashton trans.) (London: Routledge & Kegan Paul, 1973), p. 303.

212 The aphorism's closeness to the prologue of the *Origin* is also philological. The terminological coinage used here, *gedrängte Fülle*, is the same that we find in *The Origin of German Tragic Drama*, p. 32. [In the English translation it is given as 'the fullness of concentrated positivity'.]

213 Benjamin, 'One-Way Street' in *SW*, VOL. 1, p. 466.

Against the *hybris* of conceptual systemization, Benjamin does not propose abandoning oneself to the narrow embrace of the finite. The infinity of interpretation buds only in the germinative density of the most miniscule seed of truth.

> The idea is a monad—the pre-stabilized representation of phenomena resides within it, as in their objective interpretation [. . .] And so the real world could well constitute a task, in the sense that it would be a question of penetrating so deeply into everything real as to reveal thereby an objective interpretation of the world.[214]

214 Benjamin, *The Origin of German Tragic Drama*, pp. 47–48.

CHAPTER TWO

Towards a Philosophy of Language

1. Concept, idea, name

The discussion of the relation of this philosophy of interpretation to the legacy of Neo-Kantian epistemology centres on the question of the two poles of knowledge. The early text on the 'Program' had delineated as its goal the overcoming of the chasm between subject and object, understood as metaphysically opposed. Such a result seems to have become concretely attainable, for Benjamin, in the project of a critique of reason capable of encompassing the relation between its method and its theory, and therefore the relation of the investigating subject with the investigated object. The Goethean motto on the frontispiece of the *Origin* synthesizes this point of arrival with the assertion that the unity of knowing and reflection must configure 'science as an art'. That is, 'since art is always wholly represented in every individual work of art, so science ought to reveal itself completely in every individual object treated.'[1] This is exactly the idea as monad.

It is not merely that the historical event is thereby fixed, and becoming is reduced to being. If the totality is not given in a medial *continuum*, but is unleashed by singular extremes, the idea-monad will have character of the image. 'The idea is monad. The being that enters into it, with its past and subsequent history, bring—concealed in its own form—an indistinct abbreviation of the rest of the world of ideas.'[2] But the image

1 Johann Wolfgang von Goethe, *Schriften zur Naturwissenschaft* in *Sämtliche Werke*, VOL. 2 (Stuttgart and Berlin: Cotta Nachfolger, 1907), 140ff (cited in Benjamin, *Origin of German Tragic Drama*, p. 27).

2 Benjamin, *The Origin of German Tragic Drama*, p. 47.

is more than the merely conceptual, as is already expressed by the name of the faculty that Benjamin posits at the base of his discovery: fantasy. The intensive infinity that defines the monad attributes totality to it alone. The idea is monadological because it is 'imposed by totality in contrast to its own inalienable isolation.'[3] It is exactly this that opposes it to the concept, because the knowledge based on the concept 'is concerned with individual phenomena, but not directly with their unity.'[4] Unity withdraws from the direct gaze of conceptual intention which, in the effort to assert its unquestioned primacy, does not occupy itself with what in phenomena flees from its claim to identity. Only interpolation into the infinitely small is able to turn to that which is more individuated, and in this way to make a claim of totality. That being extraneous to presentness [*presenzialità*] which becomes part of the idea-monad 'brings—concealed in its own form—an indistinct abbreviation of the rest of the world of ideas, just as, according to Leibniz's *Discourse on Metaphysics* (1686), every single monad contains, in an indistinct way, all the others.'[5]

A review written in these same years fixed in the same terms the ideal of an authentic literary criticism opposed to one that was practiced falsely. Of the latter, Benjamin stated that the 'lecherous desire for the broadest perspective' is 'its cancellation.' In fact,

> the love for the object holds to the *radical singularity* of the work of art and springs from the point of creative indistinction, where penetration into the essence of the 'beautiful' or 'art' weaves into and melds with that in the work which is absolutely exceptional and unique. This advances within its interior like into that of a monad, which, as is known, has no windows but carries within itself the miniature of the whole.[6]

---

3 Benjamin, *The Origin of German Tragic Drama*, p. 47.

4 Benjamin, *The Origin of German Tragic Drama*, p. 30.

5 Benjamin, *The Origin of German Tragic Drama*, p. 47.

6 Benjamin, review of Oskar Walzel's *Das Wortkunstwerk* (7 November 1926) in *Gesammelte Schriften*, VOL. 3, p. 51.

Not only is the idea-monad the true and proper nucleus of the subsequent theory of 'images in thought', but its vertiginous inexhaustibility seems to constitute itself, for Benjamin, through a game of mirrors, like the rhythmic widening rings of water in a pond when a stone is tossed in. Nothing is more characteristic, in this sense, than the interpretation of Goethe's *Elective Affinities* in light of the novella contained within it and narrated by one of the novel's protagonists. Benjamin allows no element of it to escape him, because,

> with regard to the freedom and necessity that it reveals vis-a-vis the novel, the novella is comparable to an image in the darkness of a cathedral—an image which portrays the cathedral itself, and so in the midst of the interior communicates a view of the place that is not otherwise available.[7]

In the idea as monad, we definitively witness the introduction of the image into the conceptual element. The being of the realm of ideas can never be seen otherwise than in terms of this figurative allusiveness. The wellspring of all images can never be anything other than the ungraspable point for any intention oriented toward metaphor. According to the great intuition of Benjamin's philosophy of the name, such an intention can flourish only thanks to 'the blissful yearning that has already crossed the threshold of image and possession, and knows only the power of the name [. . .] and, imageless, is the refuge of all images.'[8]

The discovery of the inexhaustible figurative reserves of the idea-monad appears to achieve its fulfilment in the destruction of epistemology, which is the true theme of the prologue to the book on the baroque. At the same time, this liquidation of any merely classificatory conceptual formation is the testing ground for an alternative philosophy of language.

The critique of the theory of knowledge means the critique of the process of abstraction. This involves both the conception of truth as a system for cataloguing categories and the confusion of the idea with the

7 Benjamin, 'Goethe's *Elective Affinities*' in *SW*, VOL. 1, p. 352.

8 Walter Benjamin, 'Short Shadows (I)' in *SW*, VOL. 2, PART 1, p. 269.

concept understood as the mark of that which it subsumes. In the domain of knowledge, the arrangement of concepts is governed by the principle of subsumption. Just as the phenomenon to be known, once known, loses its self-subsistence and remains a mere residue to be expunged, in the same way, a hierarchy of sub-concepts is elaborated in which concepts refer upward to higher-grade concepts, and so on. Every super-concept constitutes itself as the medium of a grouping of similar phenomena which render themselves available according to how they are organized, precisely in the dimension of a 'class' or a 'genre'. This is made possible by abstracting thought, which, within the confines of language, assimilates the concept to the abstraction of the designating sign, eliminating any trace of the true nature of the word. The 1916 essay on language had grasped—in its rigorous purification of the concept from any mimetic element—the thread of the pitiless domination that man exercises over nature in the very attempt to emancipate himself from nature's domination. 'The abstract elements of language [. . .] are rooted in the word of judgement. The immediacy [. . .] of the communicability of abstraction resides in judgement.' The abstract concept thus posits itself as the true consequence of Adam's sin:

> This immediacy in the communication of abstraction came into being as judgement, when, in the Fall, man abandoned immediacy in the communication of the concrete—that is, name, and fell into the abyss of the mediateness of all communication, of the word as means, of the empty word, into the abyss of prattle.[9]

But nothing is more fragile than the organization which the word, degenerated to a means, presumes to confer arbitrarily on the world. The objectivity of any conceptual construction has as its criterion the rigorous chain of its deductions, never the reference to the object, however this may be constituted. To recognize the being of things only in the degree to which being qualifies as certain means constructing objective reality according to the dimensions of the subject that tyrannizes it. It is natural,

---

9 Benjamin, 'On Language as Such and on the Language of Man' in *SW*, VOL. 1, p. 72.

given these presuppositions, that the history of logic ends up with nominalism, which declares the abstract universal a mere *flatus vocis*, an arbitrary creation.

Any characterization of the relation of philosophy with experience is forged in the consideration of the choice between nominalism and realism. Benjamin's realm of ideas does not evade this confrontation, and the originality of the position he takes in this regard is of a piece with the singular vindication of the linguistic nature of truth. The complexity of Benjamin's argumentation has led many an interpreter to misunderstand the strength of his solution. The first to have taken this path was Adorno himself, in the 1955 Introduction to Benjamin's *Schriften*. His misstep begins with the intuition—correct so far as it goes—that, in Benjamin's philosophy, the fortress where subjectivity claimed its domain has collapsed. But in Adorno's exegesis, this is not configured as the result of a well-defined orientation of thought. 'Paradoxically', Benjamin's speculative method would encounter the empirical method, resulting in a 'metaphysical rescue of nominalism' undertaken quite inductively and yet 'in an eccentric manner'.[10] The blunder is evident, in general because it misunderstands the real scope of Benjamin's speculations in this regard, and in particular because it misreads the pages in the *Origin* specifically devoted to nominalism.

And yet Benjamin renders very clearly his position with regard to the nominalism of Jacob Burckhardt's *Kulturgeschichte* (cultural history):

> The correctness of such an attitude is evident, inasmuch as it is opposed to the hypostatization of general concepts—although this does not include universals in all their forms. But it is a quite inadequate response to a Platonic theory of science, whose aim is the representation of essences, for it fails to appreciate its necessity.[11]

---

10 Adorno, *Über Walter Benjamin*, pp. 36–37.

11 Benjamin, *The Origin of German Tragic Drama*, p. 40.

Certainly, the theory of knowledge cannot do without nominalism, but nominalism's limits are the limits of the world of science. Adorno's misunderstanding is based on the fact that, in practice, nominalism takes as its object the empirical and facticity, which in any realism are simply ignored. But the preoccupation with absolute certainty that saturates all modern empiricism, and the shifting of accent towards the subject, continuously tend to reduce to nothing the proclaimed requirement of fealty to the object. The empiricist nominalism of metaphysics as a science is always at the point of flipping over into the realism of the subject who knows, into the realism of its abstractions, which is to say into realism *tout court*. This is no different, moreover, from the way in which any realist metaphysics, precisely by determining its entities starting from the methodological procedure of the formation of concepts, comes to terms with the nominalism it sets itself up against. What Benjamin seeks instead is the point of equilibrium between these extremes, which flip continuously into one another. As always, this is the concept derived from Goethe—definitively assimilated by Benjamin ever since the composition of his dissertation—according to which the 'given fact' and 'theory' are not two opposed poles but rather are only 'two expressions and factors of a unified and irreducible relation.'[12] If we wish to speak of a nominalism in Benjamin with regard to his proposal to 'rescue' phenomena, it can be done only at the price of the extravagant impropriety of a nominalism whose foundation is not subjectivity. Few, in fact, have criticized as scathingly as Benjamin the epistemological process that extirpates any peculiarity of phenomena to reduce them to their abstract concepts. He sees no value in the received nominalist view according to which empiricity is the world of chaos awaiting the ordering illumination of the subject, brute matter waiting to be manipulated and constructed according to the caprice of the one who turns it to use. The domination of nature must be replaced by reliance on it, by concordance with it, because things have an identity of their own which is not to be dissolved but—if knowledge is to become truth—must be encouraged.

12 Cassirer, 'Idea of Metamorphosis and Idealistic Morphology: Goethe', p. 145.

The link between universals and ideas is given by the fact that the idea of *Trauerspiel* as literary genre, the focus of the *Origin*, is precisely a universal. A universal can thus not be thought of, for Benjamin, as the product of an 'uncritical use of inductive methods'.[13] Its realm, that of the idea, is entirely peculiar. We have seen that the idea-monad has a plastic character, such that the behaviour adequate to grasping it would seem to be that of vision, of the 'intuition of essences' in the Husserlian sense. But for Benjamin, 'it is not a question here of the actualization of images in visual terms; rather, in philosophical contemplation, the idea is released from the heart of reality as the word, reclaiming its name-giving rights.'[14] What brings the idea to light is not intuitive vision, but rather the production of a linguistic nexus.

Benjamin is convinced, in fact, that,

> every truth has its home, its ancestral palace, in language; and that this palace is constructed out of the oldest *logoi*; and that the insights of individual bodies of knowledge remain subordinate to truth grounded in this way, as long as they haphazardly resort to things from the sphere of language, like nomads, as it were, caught up in the view of the symbolic nature of language, which marks their terminology with the most irresponsible arbitrariness. Philosophy, in contrast, knows the blessed efficiency of an order, by virtue of which its insights always strive for very specific words whose surface has been hardened in the concept but dissolves when it comes into contact with the magnetic force of this order, revealing the forms of linguistic life locked within. But for the writer, this relationship signifies the good fortune of possessing the touchstone of his intellectual power in the language that unfolds like this before his eyes.[15]

---

13 Benjamin, *The Origin of German Tragic Drama*, p. 39.

14 Benjamin, *The Origin of German Tragic Drama*, p. 37.

15 Letter to Hugo von Hofmannstahl, 13 January 1924, in Benjamin, *Correspondence*, pp. 228–29.

Above all else, the word of the poet is what founds such ideas if they do not locate themselves in that stratum of language which is a sign system. They cannot be produced arbitrarily, because they offer themselves up only 'in a primordial form of perception, in which words possess their own nobility as names, unimpaired by cognitive meaning.'[16]

The point of indifferentiation between nominalism and realism thus qualifies itself concretely as the sphere of the linguistic 'middle ground'. Signifier and signified cannot be reciprocally indifferent to one another. Logical content needs a linguistic support that philosophy must track down in reality itself, by listening to it. From another point of view, we can characterize the attribution of autonomy to language, as opposed to the isolation of an absolute sphere of signifying, as privileging the realm of the name over that of the sign. This distinction is presented in a note, drafted probably in connection with a reading of Heidegger's work on Duns Scotus:

> The sign never refers necessarily to the signified; it therefore never refers to the object, because the object makes itself accessible only to a necessary, inward intention. The sign refers to what signifies the object; it denotes that which signifies the object. It denotes, for example, the word 'triangle' or the mathematical drawing of a triangle (mathematical objects are not signified by words alone) [. . .] The name 'triangle' does not exist in the language any more than there are names for most objects. The language has words only for those objects within which names lie concealed. By the power of names, words have their intention towards objects; they participate in objects through names. The name does not exist in them in a pure form, but is bound to a sign [. . .] The name is the analogue of the knowledge of the object in the object itself. The object divides into name and essence. The name is supra-essence; it signifies the relation of the object to its essence.[17]

---

16 Benjamin, *The Origin of German Tragic Drama*, p. 36.

17 Walter Benjamin, 'The Object: Triangle' in *SW*, VOL. 1, p. 91.

Just as the Kantian terminology in the 'Program' vindicated the concrete contents of transcendental philosophy, the phenomenological conceptual apparatus critiques itself and dissolves. The intentionality of the sign stands only through the individuation of a setting that transcends the relation of the signifier with what it designates, and thus with any intentionality. This supra-essential realm, which institutes the infinite dispositions of the sign with regard to its object, is that of the name. By the strength of its foundational character, this sphere withdraws from any immediate, definitive encounter with any type of intentional relation, even an intuitional one.

> Truth is not an intent which realizes itself in empirical reality; it is the power which determines the essence of this empirical reality. The state of being, beyond all phenomenality, to which alone this power belongs, is that of the name. This determines the manner in which ideas are given.[18]

At the base of the determination of the idea of the *Trauerspiel* stand the actual works of the baroque poets, the dramas of Gryphius, Lohenstein, Hallmann. The idea of the *Trauerspiel*, as we have said, is not that of a genre that claims 'to encompass "under" itself a number of given works of literature on the basis of certain features that are common to them'.[19] Rather, it is itself a structure 'at the very least equal in consistency and substance to any and every drama, without being in any way commensurable.'[20] The treatment of the nexus between artworks and the idea as an 'originary relation' has thus traced out a first distinct border between this type of 'universal' and any merely classificatory concept. A result of all the preceding analyses is the prohibition on speaking of the idea in terms of a 'reality' having the factual, thingly character of a presence. What is peculiar to it instead is a virtual essence, the need, in order to achieve realization, of a moment of representation. The idea does not have the realistic aspect of a 'being-available' [*essere a disposizione*]. Its

---

18 Benjamin, *The Origin of German Tragic Drama*, p. 36.

19 Benjamin, *The Origin of German Tragic Drama*, p. 44 (translation modified).

20 Benjamin, *The Origin of German Tragic Drama*, p. 44.

character is not determined as property, in the sense that knowledge possesses its objects. 'For the thing possessed, representation is secondary; it does not have prior existence as something representing itself. But the opposite holds good of truth.'[21] As a realm of truth and a refuge of the name, the realm of ideas in the book on the baroque can be grasped only in terms of its capacity to bring to light the essence of the phenomena we observe. Any quality of substantiality must be withdrawn from the idea. It this way, as a bearer of truth—both in its being and in its way of offering itself—it differentiates itself from all other worldly entities. 'Ideas are not among the given elements of the world of phenomena. This gives rise to the question of the manner in which they are in fact given.'[22] A preliminary to this latter specification, however, is a full comprehension of the relation that binds the idea to such a world. The description of this relation must also consider the specific way in which Benjamin's 'saving the phenomena' takes place.

Ideas do not come into the world as exemplars or archetypes of entities, which is to say they are not susceptible to direct representation but require the mediation of the concepts and phenomena which they subsume. 'For ideas are not represented in themselves, but solely and exclusively in an arrangement of concrete elements in the concept: as the configuration of these elements.'[23] The relation between ideas and things thus presents no affinities with its traditional interpretation in a neo-platonic sense, according to which the relation has the character of immediacy, and phenomena are seen in a polar relation to their 'entity-ized' abstractions. 'The idea thus belongs to a fundamentally different world from that which it apprehends.'[24] In the prologue to his book on the baroque, Benjamin, in fact, never oscillates between speculative absolutism and immersion in raw empiria. He indicates very clearly that the diverse realms of ideas and the elements that constitute them are

---

21 Benjamin, *The Origin of German Tragic Drama*, p. 29.

22 Benjamin, *The Origin of German Tragic Drama*, p. 35.

23 Benjamin, *The Origin of German Tragic Drama*, p. 34.

24 Benjamin, *The Origin of German Tragic Drama*, p. 34.

not detached, but hover in a precise equilibrium: 'Ideas are to objects as constellations are to stars. This means, in the first place, that they are neither their concepts nor their laws.'[25] For Benjamin, ideas, 'do not contribute to the knowledge of phenomena, and in no way can the latter be criteria with which to judge the existence of ideas.'[26] Ideas do not annex phenomena but constitute only the light in whose reflection phenomena may come to be interpreted. Benjamin's idea constitutes an ulterior background with respect to what it preserves, belonging 'to a fundamentally different world from that which it apprehends.'[27] Such a consideration accommodates the requirements of the habitual way of approaching phenomena, which is to say the cognitive process as usually understood. It is not the case that ideas, in their dimension as constellations, ascend to a role capable of rendering more correct epistemological claims. For Benjamin, it is properly and uniquely concepts that unify phenomena:

> Phenomena do not, however, enter into the realm of ideas whole, in their crude empirical state, adulterated by appearances, but only in their basic elements, redeemed. They are divested of their false unity so that, thus divided, they might partake of the genuine unity of truth. In this their division, phenomena are subordinate to concepts.[28]

The specific mode of the rescue of phenomena here actuated thus positions itself totally outside the traditional alternative between immanence and transcendence, because ideas, just as they are not concepts into which things resolve themselves integrally, are also not the laws that regulate them. 'Ideas are timeless constellations, and by virtue of the elements being seen as points in such constellations, phenomena are subdivided and at the same time redeemed.'[29] The term 'constellation'

---

25 Benjamin, *The Origin of German Tragic Drama*, p. 34.

26 Benjamin, *The Origin of German Tragic Drama*, p. 34.

27 Benjamin, *The Origin of German Tragic Drama*, p. 34.

28 Benjamin, *The Origin of German Tragic Drama*, p. 33.

29 Benjamin, *The Origin of German Tragic Drama*, p. 34.

should be granted the most real possible value. It is not the circumscription of a Kantian realm of absolute validity, uncontaminated and far from the vicissitudes of the empiria. Rather it is an effectual force field which from time to time finds its magnetic concretions in a detail. As such, it can never be immobilized in its integral determination and it will never allow itself to be met by a cognitive intention. 'The structure of truth, then, demands a mode of being which in its lack of intentionality resembles the simple existence of things, but which is superior in its permanence.'[30]

2. Word and poetry

The givenness of ideas cannot take place except by establishing, through listening, a relation with their being that strives to form the divine name, withdrawn from any phenomenality even as it nourishes it from its hidden reserves. The ineffability of this transcendence will never know a fulgurating disclosure, in the enraptured vision of a realm of purported evidence. The rejection of the notion of evidence, beyond its polemical implications with regard to phenomenology, is in Benjamin a result of Romantic epistemology. The assumption in the *Origin* of Goethe's formula combining knowledge and reflection is in fact nothing other than a variant echo of the Romantic search for intuition devoid of evidence. It is significant that, as in the *Origin*, the givenness of ideas is determined in the sphere of the name. In the dissertation, the Romantics are credited for discovering that a type of non-intellectual intuition, refractory towards states of ecstasy, is accessible only in language. 'Terminology is the sphere in which thought moves beyond discursivity and demonstrability.'[31] For the Romantics, the embryo of the system is contained in the term, in the concept; its entirety is, so to speak, preformed. 'Schlegel's thinking is absolutely conceptual—that is, it is linguistic thinking.'[32] From this presupposition derives the general tendency of Schlegel, Novalis, and

30 Benjamin, *The Origin of German Tragic Drama*, p. 36.

31 Benjamin, 'Concept of Criticism in German Romanticism' in *SW*, VOL. 1, p. 140.

32 Benjamin, 'Concept of Criticism in German Romanticism' in *SW*, VOL. 1, p. 140.

Schleiermacher to loosen the rigor of the deductive process in the search for a 'mystical terminology'. The play of contrasts and resemblances with Benjamin is here quite revelatory. In Schlegel, in fact, the terminological linguistic process, as founded on the hypothesis of a continuous medial nexus in conceptual reflection, gives birth to an uninterrupted series of new terminological coinings, and the absolute lends itself to repeated and ever-new denominations. For Benjamin, on the contrary, 'in the course of its history [. . .] philosophy is—and rightly so—a struggle for the representation of a limited number of words which always remain the same—a struggle for the representation of ideas.'[33] Goethe's anti-Romantic polemic thus reactivates itself, in its basic contents, in a singular interweaving with the peculiar requirements of linguistic speculation. Benjamin, in fact, has taken the precept according to which the ideal of art manifests itself in a limited harmonic discontinuity of pure contents and welded it with his desire to retrace the originary identity of the idea and the name. Adamitic naming had been ignored by the early Romantics precisely because in 'their speculations truth assumed the character of a reflective consciousness in place of its linguistic character.'[34] The discontinuous finitude of the realm of ideas allows itself to be configured as something more than the mere result of the doctrine of originary phenomena, which are destined to segment themselves monadologically due to their intensive infinity.

The intangible autonomy of the idea is determined, more consequentially, as the fruit of its linguistic nature. This character of the idea had only been lightly touched upon by the Jena Romantics who, while grasping the correct requirement not to transgress the moment of representation in truth, had wasted it by subordinating that moment to the necessity of expressing the infinite movement of reflection.

It can be said that for Benjamin, even if the Romantics had duly recognized the formal side of language, they had not known how to see its specific content, reductively leading it back to the dimension of

---

33 Benjamin, *Origin of German Tragic Drama*, p. 37.

34 Benjamin, *Origin of German Tragic Drama*, p. 38.

knowledge. And yet such content is precisely the moment of the primordial truth in language: 'it is that element of the symbolic in the essence of any word.'[35] The isolation of the profane element of language, relegated to the realm of communication, leads in this way to the divinization of words which thereby erects the throne of the idea. The task of philosophical representation is to restore the originary denominative value of verbal expression, which is effected by putting its symbolic valence to work.

The impulse that Benjamin's interrogation communicates to the word aims at shaking up its signifying and referential residue to bring to light its naked symbolic being, as the place 'in which the indissoluble and necessary bonding of truth content to material content appears.'[36] This unity may not be configured in any other way, because the link that binds—in the symbolic point—the sensible with the supra-sensible element can never be directly produced, in the same way that it flees from any 'actualization of images in visual terms.'[37] The reference to the ineffable dimension of the name stands, in fact, as we have seen, on the presumption of its ineradicable distance from any figurability, and thus on the hypothesis that it can only be displayed symbolically. It is not that the name is the mere essence of the image, a simple *nihil negativum*; rather, it is the seat of any image, the source from which images may flow. 'In the name, the mental being of man communicates itself to God.'[38] The absolute infinity of the divine word and its creative import, in which humankind participates, are the only guarantee capable of keeping language from collapsing into the muteness to which any logical absolutism condemns it, by which the object nullifies itself without residue into that which signifies it. The fetishization of the signified as a

---

35 Benjamin, *The Origin of German Tragic Drama*, p. 36.

36 Benjamin, 'Goethe's *Elective Affinities*' in *SW*, VOL. 1, p. 318.

37 Benjamin, *The Origin of German Tragic Drama*, p. 37.

38 Benjamin, 'On Language as Such and on the Language of Man' in *SW*, VOL. 1, p. 65. [In Carchia's translation, 'mental being' is rendered 'l'essere spirituale dell'uomo' (the spiritual being of man). —Trans.]

realized universal, which takes place, for example, in the realm of phenomenology, prescribes for phenomena a completely laid out communicative realm, which phenomena must simply fit into. But this immobilization of the dialectic process which, in reality, supports the relations of the signified with the myriad senses that the world discloses, is not only illusory but, if it were ever actually to take place, it would destroy the very possibility of language. To safeguard against such a possibility, Benjamin calls for a humble attitude on the part of anyone who would interrogate reality, rather than overwhelming it. Only 'in philosophical contemplation, the idea is released from the heart of reality as the word, reclaiming its name-giving rights.'[39]

Here is achieved and detailed the aim that Benjamin seemed to have set for himself since the text on the 'Program', the goal of the effectual overcoming of the subjectivism that deforms the Kantian theory of knowledge. 'The great transformation and correction which must be performed upon the concept of knowledge, oriented so one-sidedly along mathematical-mechanical lines, can be attained only by relating knowledge to language, as was attempted by Hamann during Kant's lifetime.'[40] It was precisely in his having pursued the speculative line of Hamann and Humboldt that Scholem identified the great merit of Benjamin, just as the latter, by abandoning the 'metaphysics of language', seemed to turn his interests towards the pole of Marxist materialism.[41] This is not a matter of a generic inheritance, as is often supposed. In particular, the relation with Hamann should be made as detailed and concrete as possible, because the reception of Hamann's formulation, which posits language as an organ and criterion of reason, had come to Benjamin by a distinctly eccentric channel.

This aspect of Benjamin's speculation can be traced to the general background of his insight into the relation between nature and history.

---

39 Benjamin, *The Origin of German Tragic Drama*, p. 37.

40 Benjamin, 'On the Program of the Coming Philosophy' in *SW*, VOL. 1, pp. 107–8.

41 See Gerhard Scholem's letter to Benjamin, 30 March 1931, in Benjamin, *Correspondence*, p. 374.

'Words, along with mathematical signs, are the only means of expression available to science, and they are not signs.'[42] But this peculiar character of the word, which goes beyond its most obvious connotation as *Zeichen* (sign), can come into focus only through the analysis of its mimetic dimension. The logical categorization of this layer of the word seems to reveal itself, at the same time, as an insertion into the perspective of temporal unfolding. Because in the hypothesis that 'language may be seen as the highest level of mimetic behaviour and the most complete archive of non-sensuous similarity,' language would be nothing but 'a medium into which the earlier powers of mimetic production and comprehension have passed without residue, to the point where they have liquidated those of magic.'[43] But the 'historicization' of this aspect of language that Benjamin puts into effect should not be misunderstood. Everything depends on comprehending the true value of his resolute affirmation that 'the primary problem of language is its magic.'[44] Benjamin does not at all intend to claim the indiscriminate unity of mankind with nature, enacted in sympathetic magic, as something opposed to the absolute liberty of the fully open spirit, as may be found in Hegel's premise to his discussion of the unfolding of the subjective spirit, the natural soul and sentient soul, envisaged as the lowest steps in the anthropological scale. That magic constitutes the originary pole of language can be explained in the sense that it is posited as a moment of authenticity in the dimension of the word. Benjamin labours to salvage this 'magic' configuration of language. The interest bestowed on Hamann's conception is thus justified in light of its 'magical' orientation.

In the famous academy described by Jonathan Swift in *Gulliver's Travels* (PART 3, CHAPTER 5), the wise men proposed the total abolition of words and their substitution, for conversational purposes, with the things which they denote. This delightful fable has mostly been interpreted, within the framework of contemporary philosophy of language, as an

---

42 Benjamin, *The Origin of German Tragic Drama*, p. 42.

43 Walter Benjamin, 'On the Mimetic Faculty' in *SW*, VOL. 2, PART 2, p. 722.

44 Benjamin, 'On Language as Such and on the Language of Man' in *SW*, VOL. 1, p. 64.

indirect confirmation of Russell's theory of denotation, whose ideal form would be a language of this sort, in which only syntax exists and vocabulary is absent, or as a humorous actualization of Wittgenstein's realism in the propositions of the *Tractatus*. Benjamin's theory of language seems to allow for a different exegesis of Swift's hypothesis. In this case, behind the proposal of the Lagado school of languages would lie the conviction that there exists a symbolism of the concrete that comes before any human effort of signification. From this perspective, the particular experience of every thing has a meaning, even when no symbols intervene to explicate it. The only condition is that the living creature be awake and full of sensibility. Even in the stone, 'the lowest stratum of created things,' we must be able to descry, as happens in Leskov, 'a natural prophecy of petrified, lifeless nature concerning the historical world.'[45]

> The language of an entity is the medium in which its mental being is communicated. The uninterrupted flow of this communication runs through the whole of nature, from the lowest forms of existence to man and from man to God.[46]

Only a language such as that of mathematics has been capable of freeing itself from any residue of this natural symbolism of things. In all other languages, including the most abstract hieroglyphic writing, this type of concrete representation is latent, in which every being directly expresses itself. On the other hand, the task of mankind to name things would fail, because

> It would be insoluble, were not the name-language of man and the nameless language of things related in God and released from the same creative word, which in things became the communication of matter in magic communion, and in man the language of knowledge and name in blissful mind.[47]

---

45 Walter Benjamin, 'The Storyteller: Observations on the Works of Nikolai Leskov' in *SW*, VOL. 3, p. 161.

46 Benjamin, 'On Language as Such and on the Language of Man' in *SW*, VOL. 1, p. 74.

47 Benjamin, 'On Language as Such and on the Language of Man' in *SW*, VOL. 1, p. 70.

This affinity of things is 'magic' because it alone makes possible the immediacy of any spiritual communication in the adequate form impressed on it by the concept of immaterial resemblance. 'There is, in the relation of human languages to that of things, something that can be approximately described as "overnaming".'[48] In the language of mankind, things suffer the abundance of their names. Such a linguistic 'surplus' is the result of the magic of the word, whose power induces, in the ego of humans, the temptation to inflate to grotesque proportions this patrimony of theirs which is so easy to acquire. For this reason, overnaming is certainly 'the deepest linguistic reason for all melancholy and (from the point of view of the thing) for all deliberate muteness.'[49] But at the same time, sadness, as testimony of the impossibility to grasp the unique divine name, declares, as we've seen, that this inexhaustible overnaming is the only condition for inter-human communication. This 'opulence' of names theorized by Benjamin could be translated into the formulas of the science that investigates the phenomena of wealth. We will then find ourselves facing the only economic system in history in which the inexhaustible capacity for production has no need that the demand for names be equally unlimited. The unconsumed reserves, quite exceptionally, have no deleterious effect on the ever-renewing production.

The terms of the problem do not change if we refer, rather than to this youthful work, to Benjamin's later reflections on language.

In a *Referat* (report) drafted in 1935 for the Institut für Sozialforschung, the focus centres entirely on the question of the relation between language and society, which had already been touched upon indirectly in the discussion of the magic element in language. It would seem inconceivable for any sociology of language to deal with the word in any other way than that of its dimension as a medium of interhuman communication. So much the more singular, then, appear the consequences that Benjamin draws from his new, materialistic attention to

---

48 Benjamin, 'On Language as Such and on the Language of Man' in *SW*, VOL. 1, p. 73.

49 Benjamin, 'On Language as Such and on the Language of Man' in *SW*, VOL. 1, p. 73.

these phenomena. It is no simple matter to find a univocal thread in this essay on the 'Problems in the Sociology of Language', one of the most extreme demonstrations of the method of literary composition inaugurated by his 1929 essay on surrealism. The principle of allegory is here condensed, in fact, into the extreme allusiveness of speaking through citations, and an autonomous conceptual direction can sustain itself only by leaning for support on an incredible abundance of references. The review, which documents a truly vast range of knowledge (from Bühler to Cassirer, from Bally and De Saussure to Carnap, from Piaget to Tolman) leaves but little space for the expression of a subjective theorization. And yet this simple function of making links that Benjamin limits himself to is enough to allow us to discern his real speculative intention. Yet again, it is a matter of putting into maximum relief that 'ancient truth' that language is not an instrument. But what is singular is that this truth no longer reveals itself to Benjamin only in philosophical reflection. What is decisive instead is precisely the fact that it must manifest itself to the student of language during the course of any inductive investigation in a field of specialized research. In this sense, Benjamin can claim, at the end of his essay, that the vision that 'stands, expressly or tacitly, at the inception of the sociology of language,'[50] has revealed itself in an exemplary manner in the language model set up by Kurt Goldstein during his research into aphasia. In light of this study,

> One could not find a better example to demonstrate how wrong it is to regard language as an instrument. What we have seen is the form in which language emerges in cases where it can be no more than an instrument. Even in the case of normal people, it can happen that language is used only as an instrument [. . .] But this instrumental function presupposes that language is really something quite different, just as it was for the patient before his or her illness [. . .] As soon as human beings use language to establish a living relationship to themselves and to others, language is no longer an instrument, no longer a means,

50 Walter Benjamin, 'Problems in the Sociology of Language' in *SW*, VOL. 3, p. 86.

> but a manifestation, a revelation of our innermost being and of the psychic bond linking us to ourselves and to our fellow human beings.[51]

If, as the final draft of the essay on Baudelaire argues, the destruction of the 'aura' signifies above all that the expectation implicit in any human gaze—'that it will be returned by that on which it is bestowed'[52]—will be disappointed, we must admit that this is precisely the case of the word reduced to a means of communication. The word here no longer reacts to the urgings of the speaker, who ends up establishing with it a one-way relation devoid of any receptive moment. Benjamin's philosophy of language instead depends distinctly on the capacity to recognize and guarantee this element of the word, as a realm where its movement is autonomous. 'Certain minds which love mystery like to believe that objects preserve something of the eyes which have looked at them.'[53] Benjamin includes himself among these lovers. And not for nothing did those who became close to him discern in him, 'a visionary whose imagery was as rich as Isaiah's', drawn to 'images of an occult world that often imposed itself as the only solution.'[54] In the same sense, Adorno observed that in Benjamin, 'words and writing', even while receiving their force from evidence, 'had the resonance of the secret.'[55] Still more, in the 1934 essay on Karl Kraus, in the heart of his 'materialistic' period, Benjamin expresses in the most comprehensive manner the dimensions of a linguistic hermeneutics sustained solely by the strength of the existence, in the word, of these 'mysterious' levels, summoned to reveal themselves to the loving gaze of the person exploring them. In the aphoristic

51 Kurt Goldstein, 'L'analyse de l'aphasie et l'étude de l'essence du langage' in *Psychologie du langage* (Paris: Félix Alcan, 1933), pp. 495–96. Cited in Benjamin, 'Problems in the Sociology of Language' in *SW*, VOL. 3, pp. 85–86.

52 Benjamin, 'On Some Motifs in Baudelaire' in *SW*, VOL. 4, p. 338.

53 Marcel Proust, *Time Regained* (Stephen Hudson trans.) (London: Chatto & Windus, 1931), p. 224; cited in 'Some Motifs in Baudelaire' in *SW*, VOL. 4, p. 338–39.

54 Pierre Klossowski, 'Letter on Walter Benjamin (1952)' (Christian Hite trans.), *Parrhesia* 19 (2014): 14–21; here, p. 17.

55 Adorno, *Über Walter Benjamin*, p. 34.

Kraus, Benjamin found welcomed, in exemplary manner, the need to recognize the moment of the awakening in inert nature of 'medialized' language.[56]

The polemic towards the discursive and informational character of the word is the constellation under which Kraus undertakes the great battle against journalism, in which he recognized the epochal quality of having led to the victory of the *Umgangsprache*, a salient element of the deformation of human nature, the outcome of the heedless technologizing of the world inaugurated by bourgeois civilization. The resonance of this struggle harmonized singularly with Benjamin's aversion to any 'bourgeois' conception of language to the point of melding into it, making the task of delineating necessary differences that much more difficult. Information, as a new form of communication that appears 'with the complete ascendancy of the middle class—which in fully developed capitalism has the press as one of its most important instruments'—has, as an immediate consequence, the prostitution of language.[57] Its 'expressive' dimension succumbs to the aspect that Kraus defines as 'enunciation' (*Aussage*), signifying both the end of any ideal of words *pro domo et mundo*[58] and the fixation of the communicative moment in the 'empty phrase'. While the expression of the transformed function of language is deposited in journalism, 'the empty phrase of the kind so relentlessly pursued by Kraus is the label that makes a thought marketable.'[59] Kraus's goal then is the liberation of reified language from the realm of this traffic by recuperating its origin. That Kierkegaardian trait, which the figure of Kraus seems to assimilate to himself in his indefatigable, impotent, and vain polemical ardour, can be measured still more easily in his hostility to the degradation of language inherent in 'prattle' (*Geschwätz*), as seen in the explicit parallel made by Benjamin himself.[60] Benjamin

---

56 Kraus's linguistic concepts are documented in the volumes *Die Sprache* (Munich: Kösel Verlag, 1954) and *Beim Wort genommen* (Munich: Kösel Verlag, 1955).

57 Benjamin, 'Problems in the Sociology of Language' in *SW*, VOL. 3, p. 147.

58 This is the title of one of Kraus's collections of aphorisms (1912).

59 Benjamin, 'Karl Kraus' in *SW*, VOL. 2, PART 2, p. 435.

60 Benjamin, 'Karl Kraus' in *SW*, VOL. 2, PART 2, p. 448.

too had grasped, in his earliest speculations, the unresolvable, polar duality between *Geschwätz* and the 'origin' of language: 'The question as to good and evil in the world after the Creation was empty prattle. The Tree of Knowledge stood in the garden of God not in order to dispense information on good and evil, but as an emblem of judgement over the questioner.'[61] And the creatural state of paradise was also for Benjamin the only one to suppress language as communication: 'Adam's action of naming things is so far removed from play or caprice that it actually confirms the state of paradise as a state in which there is as yet no need to struggle with the communicative significance of words.'[62]

3. Dimensions of pure language

The attempt to name the name itself, to not communicate meanings, can become incarnate nowhere but in poetry, the sphere where the word emancipates itself from the constriction of effectuality to posit itself in the absolute of its perfect transparency. Its liberation thus coincides with the assumption of a sacral character, rising into a prayer finally liberated from the magical duties that deform it in the theological-profane domain. The search for the authentic value of language interpenetrates inextricably with the intention of the poetic mission, to the point that even the methodological procedures adopted in the two cases superimpose themselves on one another. In his essay on Baudelaire, Benjamin brought to light that the wellspring of poetry is knowing how to endow a thing with the capacity to look. 'Whenever a human being, an animal, or an inanimate object thus endowed by the poet lifts up its eyes, it draws him into the distance. The gaze of nature, when thus awakened, dreams and pulls the poet after its dream.'[63] This was exactly Kraus's attitude towards the word, as condensed in the statement, cited by Benjamin in 1934, according to which, 'the more closely you look at a word, the more distantly it looks

---

61 Benjamin, 'On Language as Such and on the Language of Man' in *SW*, VOL. 1, p. 72.

62 Benjamin, *The Origin of German Tragic Drama*, p. 37.

63 Benjamin, 'On Some Motifs in Baudelaire' in *SW*, VOL. 4, p. 354n77.

back.'[64] This closeness, which will not let the word slip away, but holds it tightly to persuade it to reveal itself, expresses itself for Kraus solely in rhyme. The philosophical recognition of the originary finds its specific scenario in the lyric, whose language is rhyme: 'A word that never tells an untruth at its origin,'[65] and which therefore has its abode in the innocence and virginity of the word of the child:

> The child recognizes by rhyme that it has reached the crest of language, from which it can hear the rushing of all springs at their origin. Up there, creaturely existence is at home; after so much dumbness in the animal and so much lying in the whore, it has found its tongue in the child.[66]

The sanctification of the word to which Kraus had devoted himself never assumes in him, however, the forms of the genuine linguistic cult practiced by the George-Kreis. His language 'is the medium neither of prophecy nor of domination.'[67] This is why Benjamin said that Kraus's love for language is only a *platonische Sprachliebe* (Platonic love of language).[68]

This love, once it takes on the guise of the name, has as its ideal not possession, but gratitude. 'Thanking and dedicating—for to thank is to put feelings under a name.'[69] And yet this is only the characteristic into which the distance pertaining to this linguistic love configures itself, in which rhyme takes on the role of the element supremely contiguous to the object. 'As rhyme, it gathers the similar into its aura; as name, it stands alone and expressionless.'[70] But with this Kraus has only intuited, in the seesaw of the rhyme-name couple, the authentic dialectic of the word. For Benjamin, the attribution of the word's receptive element to

---

64 Cited in Benjamin, 'Karl Kraus' in *SW*, VOL. 2, PART 2, p. 453.

65 Cited in Benjamin, 'Karl Kraus' in *SW*, VOL. 2, PART 2, p. 451.

66 Benjamin, 'Karl Kraus' in *SW*, VOL. 2, PART 2, p. 452.

67 Benjamin, 'Karl Kraus' in *SW*, VOL. 2, PART 2, p. 451.

68 Benjamin, 'Karl Kraus' in *SW*, VOL. 2, PART 2, p. 453.

69 Benjamin, 'Karl Kraus' in *SW*, VOL. 2, PART 2, p. 453.

70 Benjamin, 'Karl Kraus' in *SW*, VOL. 2, PART 2, p. 454.

rhyme risks not sufficiently guaranteeing, or even wrecking, the legitimate claims of the realm of denomination. The excessive linguistic 'mimetism' that infects the notion of rhyme could lead to the degeneration of the delicate equilibrium that sustains the word, unleashing the arbitrary will of that pole which stands opposed to such impure confusion with nature. Still more deeply, Kraus's failure leads back, according to Benjamin, to the weakness of the theoretical support provided by his mechanical counter-positioning of nature and society, which Kraus fails to grasp in their reciprocal interpenetration. For Kraus, in fact, the redemption of the human element is not represented as 'the destiny and fulfilment of nature liberated through revolutionary change, but as an element of nature per se, of an archaic nature without history, in its pristine, primeval state.'[71]

The illusory character of this naive mythology to which Kraus fell victim (to the point that in 'One-Way Street' he is assigned a *Kriegerdenkmal*, a warrior memorial) never touched Benjamin. His opposition to any linguistic naturalism was always radical. For, if the conventionalist conception of language is mistaken in seeing the word as related to things by chance, through mere signs, no less misleading is 'the rejection of bourgeois linguistic theory by mystical linguistic theory.'[72]

The word cannot be confused with the essence of the thing, as if something of the real pertained to the linguistic element, because the thing never possesses the word in an unmediated way. Language inhabits things, certainly, but only within the folds of their latent potentiality. All that is alive—in fact any communication of spiritual content—belongs to language, but in this equivalence there also takes place, at the same time, a disengagement of all spiritual reality into successive hierarchical strata. At the lowest step of this ladder is found the most imperfect language, that of things, because to things is denied the impulse of what constitutes the essence of the linguistic principle: sound. In the muteness

---

71 Benjamin, 'Karl Kraus' in *SW*, VOL. 2, PART 2, p. 447.

72 Benjamin, 'On Language as Such and on the Language of Man' in *SW*, VOL. 1, p. 69.

of nature, the word thus lives only as a virtuality. Even if the thing was also created by the divine word, the sedimentation of its essence, unveiled in the name, cannot take place except by the liberating practice of the human word. The uninterrupted flow of material resemblances that magically traverse nature like a residue of God's creative *logos* must be transfigured in the immateriality of what is purely spiritual and has its form of symbolic existence in the ethereal character of sound. The search for the primeval valence of the word can never take the form of an obligation imposed on the speaker that the word resolve itself integrally, mimetically, into the thing. The mute magic of nature cannot bind to itself, through enchantment, the spontaneous force of the name. It can only impart on the name the jolt that the traces of the divine word irradiate into its material communicative faculty. At the same time, the refusal to assimilate itself naturalistically to phenomena sanctions, for Benjamin, the failure of any pretence at reconciliation in the purity of the name between nature deformed by things and humankind. This reconciliation cannot take place because the beatitude of human life in pure linguistic spirit came to an end quite some time ago, ever since human cognitive *hybris* rendered nature mute, after the exodus from Eden. Now 'philosophy may not presume to speak in the tones of revelation.'[73] The hypothesis of the figurability of the name must give way to the awareness that philosophical denomination is mere repetition. What's more, in the discussion of the system we have already seen that the ability to grasp it, contiguous to the type of unveiling that attains the absolute, can be rendered in no other way than symbolically. Any theological sphere of 'absolute origins' is, for Benjamin, also definitively lost. The human word can communicate with the divine name only in the sense of operating in its 'recognition', which is the seal of any search for the authentic. The allusive recall of memory, which sustains the anxiety of the ineffable in any negative theology, is thus the true procedure suitable to the foolish human effort to establish a nature finally redeemed, by returning to the language of Adam.

73 Benjamin, *The Origin of German Tragic Drama*, p. 36.

At the base of the essence of the name, there certainly resides the creativity of the divine word with which God, in calling forth the world of his emanations, also denominated himself. But when mankind begins to retrace, behind the mute affliction of things, the hidden fount of their tormented communication, and makes the archetypal *logos* the object of its penetration, this essence, in the revelatory absoluteness of the fullness of absolute meaning, even as it gives meaning to all, withdraws from the grasp of human intuition. In this way it signifies nothing, presenting itself as devoid of meaning and of any concrete content. Just as it banishes any claim of language to stand as an organ of revelation, the inaccessibility to human speech of the meaningful essence of the absolute also halts its collapse into the precipice of triumphant subjectivity which, lost in the silent sonority of things, raises its voice to impose the law of its word. If the Adamitic sphere of the name is lost once and for all, then the unresolvable conflict that seemed to divide the philosophy of language into alternative theories of speech as mimesis or as convention, must also collapse. Because, as Benjamin sees it, what disappears is the presumption common to this bifurcation of the linguistic principle, with the withering of the axiom of the signifying univocality of the real requiring, as compensation, the immobilization of the word to the rank of a perfectly conscious structure. In other words, the dualism of subject and object which corrodes the foundation of Kantian epistemology returns, for Benjamin, in the aprioristic assumption that the infinitely englobing dimension of the name would let itself be grasped, definitively, on the plain of a reductive adaptation either of the word to the thing or vice versa. The inexorability of the divine word cannot be crystalized into any intuition precisely because it is the background against which any denominating activity locates itself and takes shape. The flow of language and the reality of things do not run parallel like two opposed entities which must bend one towards the other at any cost. They are, rather, like two lakes whose waters appear to be separated by a narrow strip of land, but actually mix together and fully interpenetrate immediately below the surface of that deceptive borderline.

We must clarify the theological foundation on the basis of which this singular relation between human locution and the magic communication of nature takes on the form of a genuine dialogue. It is not without importance that the genesis of the 1916 piece on language takes place in a setting which has an 'immanent relationship to Judaism', to the extent of being almost a commentary 'on the first chapters of Genesis.'[74] Only the prohibition on calling the absolute by name, of pronouncing the word God, the 'thou shalt not make unto thee any graven image' assures, in the Jewish religion, the bond between the name and being. Only at the price of emptying out any representative character of the divine idea can the conciliation between natural magic and the disenchanting word take place. As has been repeatedly observed, this is the sole possibility for saving in language its aspect as image. The purity of the divine name, transcending any imperfect representation of it, allows for philosophy to decipher 'each image as script [and] teaches us to read from its features the admission of falseness which cancels its power and hands it over to truth. Language thereby becomes more than a mere system of signs.'[75]

As a result of the demolition of transcendental philosophy, the epistemology of interpretation posits itself, in Benjamin, not as a discovery, but as the natural outcome of the theorization of language that may rightly be called 'a philosophy of translation'.

We have seen that the human being is united to the mute language of things through the word. Given the non-uniformity of the real, hierarchized in a scale of spiritual and therefore linguistic realities, the word can never achieve that univocal fusion with the object dreamed of by the doctrine of imitation. On the other hand, however, the knowledge that the human word opens up in things

> is not spontaneous creation; it does not emerge from language in the absolutely unlimited and infinite manner of creation.

---

74 See the letter to Scholem containing the mention of the essay, 11 November 1916, in Benjamin, *Correspondence*, p. 81.

75 Max Horkheimer and Theodor W. Adorno, *Dialectic of Enlightenment: Philosophical Fragments* (Edmund Jephcott trans., Gunzelin Schmid Noerr ed.) (Stanford, CA: Stanford University Press, 2002), p. 18.

> Rather, the name that man gives to language depends on how language is communicated to him. In name, the word of God has not remained creative; it has become in one part receptive, even if receptive to language.[76]

With this, the non-thing-like, non-realistic character of the idea, its refusal to be mere 'presentness', has by now been definitively clarified. The idea is not reality, but rather the recondite meaning of things, their virtual reason, and is so precisely thanks to its particular linguistic constitution which, in order to be realized, always needs a new effort of assistance by the subject representing it, the speaker who interrogates it. Thus, in the final analysis, language is defined for Benjamin as a synthesis of receptivity and spontaneity.

> For conception and spontaneity together, which are found in this unique union only in the linguistic realm, language has its own word, and this word applies also to that conception of the nameless in the name. It is the translation of the language of things into that of man.[77]

Benjamin's philosophy of translation, as comprehensively expressed, especially in terms of semantics, in the essay 'The Task of the Translator' (published in 1923 as a preface to the version of Baudelaire's *Tableaux parisiens*), cannot be grasped in its full implications until it frees itself from any link with the ontological postulates of his early speculations on language. It is important therefore to keep firmly in mind the fundamental result: language does not consist primarily in the gift of the word—which distinguishes mankind from the other living beings—but on the contrary is identified with nothing less than 'the universal essence (*Weltwesen*), language, from which speaking derives.'[78] In this light, the concept of translation cannot be treated a posteriori, as though it were a secondary

---

76 Benjamin, 'On Language as Such and on the Language of Man' in *SW*, VOL. 1, p. 69.

77 Benjamin, 'On Language as Such and on the Language of Man' in *SW*, VOL. 1, p. 69.

78 Letter to Ernst Schoen, 17 June 1918, in Benjamin, *Correspondence*, p. 132.

derivative with respect to a presumed, preliminary, 'pure' structure of language. Only in the latter, and precisely in its deepest strata, can the concept of translation discover its own necessary foundation.

No problem could stimulate Benjamin's esoteric interests more than this one, if it is true, as has been claimed, that, 'the mystery of translatability is the mystery of our being.'[79] Benjamin's encounter with the Romantic theory of art criticism and his very profession as critic thus find their justification in the heart of a more radical conception of the world.

In light of Benjamin's incisive philosophical inspiration, a legitimation of the notion of criticism cannot take place except through the will to comprehend 'the infinitely riddling nature of translation,'[80] in its constitutional proximity to philosophizing and composing poetry. The perception of this proximity is already completely implicit in Benjamin's youthful linguistic commentary on Genesis. We have seen, in fact, how the ungraspable and yet continuously re-evoked unity of the *logos* allows for circumscribing linguistic strata that surpass the signifying and denotative valences of human speech, towards an overcoming of the temporal structure that imposes on language the rupture of that relation of simultaneity within which it necessarily places subject and object. The task of humans to name things, to carry into the name that which the name does not have, finds its objectivity guaranteed in God. This idea was sublimely expressed by Hamann: 'Everything that man heard in the beginning, saw with his eyes, and felt with his hands was the living word; for God was the word.'[81] Since God created things, the name that knows them does not invent their meaning, but finds it in the germ that the creating word has left in them, and simply 'translates' it into its superior language. In a hierarchy of spiritual levels, the entities which

---

79 Hermann Broch, *Dichten und Erkennen*, Gesannekte Werke, VOL. 6 (Zürich: Rhein Verlag, 1955).

80 Benjamin, 'Concept of Criticism in German Romanticism' in *SW*, VOL. 1, p. 154.

81 Benjamin, 'On Language as Such and on the Language of Man' in *SW*, VOL. 1, p. 70.

constitute the totality of the linguistic world reciprocally communicate their essence across this same scale. Even if the meaning of the lesser of them needs to be transferred now and again into that of the higher ones, its communicative content remains—and this is decisive—unaltered in the course of passage and is, once again, the same as that of the inferior language. 'The language of nature is comparable to a secret password that each sentry passes to the next in his own language, but the content of the password is the sentry's language itself.'[82] The rigorous purification of language from the duty to communicate contents, eternally sanctioned by identifying *logos* and knowledge in God, fixes its authentic nature in the capacity to constitute itself as a channel for the uninterrupted spiritual verbalization that animates reality. 'All higher language is a translation of lower ones, until in ultimate clarity the word of God unfolds, which is the unity of this movement made up of language.'[83]

This is an initial and still quite general approximation of that *unkommunicative Element* common to Benjamin's early writings which, according to Adorno, would be more thoroughly manifested in the essay on the 'Task of the Translator'.[84] In fact, we should regard this essay as a comprehensive interpretation of the difficulties faced by any effort to liberate ancient words from their current terminological servitude, by renewing their original life in pure linguistic spirit. We can find the remedy to this obstacle condensed in the form of a precept in the already-cited letter to Hofmannstahl:

> When insight [*die Einsicht*] really proves inadequate to dissolve the petrified conceptual armour, it will find itself tempted not only to excavate [*ausschachten*] but to mine [*erbohren*] the linguistic and intellectual depth at the bottom of such attempts, so as not to revert to the barbarism of formulas.[85]

---

82 Benjamin, 'On Language as Such and on the Language of Man' in *SW*, VOL. 1, p. 74.

83 Benjamin, 'On Language as Such and on the Language of Man' in *SW*, VOL. 1, p. 74.

84 Adorno, *Über Walter Benjamin*, p. 47.

85 Letter to Hugo von Hofmannstahl, 13 January 1924, in Benjamin, *Correspondence*, p. 229.

The price of such *Erbohren* cannot help but be the emergence into plain view of the non-communicative dimension of language. This leads to a sort of forced perspective whose 'unsophisticated pedantry [. . .] is preferable, of course, to the sovereign allure of their adulteration,' even if this method should be 'the origin of certain obscurities.'[86] The search for truth has no use for explanations that attempt to furnish causal and systematic connections, just as it must strictly avoid even the most minimal trace of empathy with its object, because such an intuition 'is not the view of the object, resolved in the idea, but that of subjective states of the recipient projected into the work.'[87] The essence and the motive of a thing should never be confused with one another. No message must communicate itself from the object of inquiry to the reader, if 'One-Way Street' is correct in its scathing admonishment that the construction of life resides 'in the power far more of facts than of convictions, and of such facts as have scarcely ever become the basis of convictions.'[88] This recognition of the non-communicative element, the emphasis directed upon it by the assumption of the method of the *Erbohren*, is rooted in profound theoretical reasoning. Only a theory of translation can explain why 'No poem is intended for the reader, no picture for the beholder, no symphony for the audience.'[89]

In the 1916 essay, the achievement of a neutral zone in language where activity and passivity cancel each other out—interpenetrating in the notion of the transferability of worldly spiritual-linguistic content—permits Benjamin literally to turn upside down the orientation that rationalistic aesthetics adopt in discussing the problem of the translatability of works of poetry. The position of these aesthetics would be much better defined, however, if one were to say that the issue simply doesn't really exist at all for them. It is evident that if we accept the distinction between thought, as an end, and language, demoted to mere means, the effectual yield of poetic content becomes the only point to

86 Letter to Hugo von Hofmannstahl, 13 January 1924, in Benjamin, *Correspondence*, p. 229.

87 Benjamin, *Origin of German Tragic Drama*, p. 42.

88 Benjamin, 'One-Way Street' in *SW*, VOL. 1, p. 444.

89 Benjamin, 'Task of the Translator' in *SW*, VOL. 1, p. 253.

be considered and presents no difficulty; it is just a banal reproduction of the merely syntactic and discursive order of a text. What constitutes the decisive element of any philosophy of translation becomes, for these theorists, an element of disturbance, something to set aside in some corner alongside personal curiosities or whims.

Saussure's *cours*, Hjelmslev's *Prologomena*, and Sapir's semantic philosophy have sufficiently proven that every language conceals in itself its own secret metaphysics, an entire vision of the world, in which the plane of the linguistic *signifier* is not something accessory and derivative that serves only to communicate and express ideas, but itself conditions and forms them. The opinion that the linguistic sign simply points to a sphere of meaning external to language is unsustainable, because that sign is actually born from the encounter between expression and content. No conceptual universal pre-exists linguistic denomination, so that the different languages regard the world, categorizing it according to irreducibly distinct schema. Without a *sprachliche Mittelwelt* (linguistic middle-world), it is impossible to weld together the diverse spiritual planes into which, for Benjamin, the real is broken up. But these *Weltbilder* (world-images) are different for each language. Translation, however, as a transposition of one language into another through a continuous series of transformations, does not measure out 'abstract areas of identity and similarity,' but rather a 'continuum of transformations.'[90] That is, the concept of resemblance is inadequate to characterize the relation of a language to the original because the content here enters into an entirely particular relation with the word. In fact, content and language constitute 'a certain unity in the original, like a fruit and its skin, the language of the translation envelops its content like a royal robe with ample folds.'[91] The translator cannot have as a purpose, as commonly believed, the restitution of the content of the original. On the contrary, the translator must stand absolutely apart from the intention to share with the reader something of the original's meaning. The original

---

90 Benjamin, 'On Language as Such and on the Language of Man' in *SW*, VOL. 1, p. 70.

91 Benjamin, 'Task of the Translator' in *SW*, VOL. 1, p. 258.

is essential to translation 'only insofar as it has already relieved the translator and the translation of the effort of assembling and expressing what is to be conveyed.'[92] It is a matter of understanding that nothing is clearer than the meaning of the original, which cannot therefore demand, in the new version, any kind of regeneration. The mutation of the work never addresses itself to that first language consigned to determining the letter of the text, but rather attempts to make the infinite objectivity of its symbolic side, which constitutes itself in the sphere of pure language, fluctuate above it. In translation,

> the original rises into a higher and purer linguistic air, as it were. It cannot live there permanently, to be sure; neither can it reach that level in every aspect of the work. Yet in a singularly impressive manner, it at least points the way to this region: the predestined, hitherto inaccessible realm of reconciliation and fulfilment of languages.[93]

Substituting her own language for that of the author, the translator may never deform the original, taking it as a pretext to express herself through it, because she is aware that her task is not to reproduce a meaning buried in the objectivity of the letter of the text. The work of translation must only prolong the signifying valence of the artwork, but never reduce or eliminate it. The language of the original is never to be considered as an object, a signified (emerging from a subject) that must be opposed to the subjectivity of the translator. It is, rather, the predicate of an activity which intends to reproduce in its own language not a message, but its symbolic condition, thereby creating not areas of resemblance, but chains of transformation, homologies of relation.

> Fragments of a vessel that are to be glued together must match one another in the smallest details, although they need not be like one another. In the same way a translation, instead of imitating the sense of the original, must lovingly and in detail incorporate the original's way of meaning, thus making both

---

92 Benjamin, 'Task of the Translator' in *SW*, VOL. 1, p. 260.

93 Benjamin, 'Task of the Translator' in *SW*, VOL. 1, p. 257.

> the original and the translation recognizable as fragments of a greater language, just as fragments are part of a vessel.[94]

If we were to substitute the traditional characterization of language as the domain of abstract concepts, where the word has a mere decorative function, by identifying it instead with truth, then the reciprocal transference of languages can no longer obey the rhetoric of the imitation of development, but rather that of variation and discontinuity.

> It is a question of showing that in cognition there could be no objectivity, not even a claim to it, if this were to consist in imitations of the real; in the former, one can demonstrate that no translation would be possible if in its ultimate essence it strove for likeness to the original. For in its afterlife [. . .] the original undergoes a change.[95]

But how can a translator attempt to reproduce, in her own version, that pure language that conditions the original, making it rotate around its invisible point, where any intention of meaning is extinguished and the word is itself a point of arrival, no longer intending or expressing anything? Benjamin himself suggests interpreting this ultimate nucleus of the original as its symbolic essence, 'depending on the context in which it appears, it is something that symbolizes or something symbolized. It is the former only in the finite products of language; the latter, in the evolving of languages themselves.'[96] It is not enough that the incommunicable symbolic profile of the original be recognized, beyond the tautological reproduction of the meaning. Its deciphering must take place in a code that has the same latent profundity as the text to be translated, and must never insist on wishing to expunge the insecurity generated by the text's infinite linguistic metaphoricity. The semantic dimension is respected by the translator, according to Benjamin, only when she compels her own language to take on the same symbolic gravity as that of the original. Or, in slightly different terms, only when

---

94 Benjamin, 'Task of the Translator' in *SW*, VOL. 1, p. 260.

95 Benjamin, 'Task of the Translator' in *SW*, VOL. 1, p. 256.

96 Benjamin, 'Task of the Translator' in *SW*, VOL. 1, p. 261.

the symbology of the text and that of its version conjugate the same verb of this inaccessible language.

> The significance of fidelity as ensured by literalness is that the work reflects the great longing for linguistic complementation. A real translation is transparent; it does not cover the original, does not block its light, but allows the pure language, as though reinforced by its own medium, to shine upon the original all the more fully.[97]

Due to its withdrawal from any cognitive task, this pure language, which lives concealed in the subtlest shadings of any translation, becomes the authentic language of truth, upon which the nostalgia of the philosopher nourishes itself. In the search for a pure language, as recondite, paradigmatic moments of his parallel between poetry and translation, Benjamin held in one hand the Schlegelian concept of the 'poetry of the poetry', and in the other the practice of Hölderlin, in which the poem concretely revealed itself in its essence as the poem of the poem.

The model of Hölderlin, in fact, inspired the earliest and yet no less astonishing of Benjamin's works, the commentary on the two poems, 'Dichtermut' ('The Poet's Courage') and 'Blödigkeit' ('Timidity'),[98] in the discovery of the radical coherence of a poetry that posits itself in essence as a theory of the poetic act. Already in this first critical exercise, Benjamin explained that the reading of the work must exhibit 'the inner form, which Goethe characterized as content (*Gehalt*) [. . .] The poetic task, as the preliminary condition of an evaluation of the poem, is to be established.' This, as a pre-condition of *Dichtung*, is to be understood as, 'the intellectual-perceptual [*geistig-anschaulich*] structure of the world to which the poem [*Gedicht*] bears witness. This task, this precondition, shall be understood here as the ultimate basis [*Grund*] accessible to analysis.' Only in such a sphere, which has a form particular to each poem and qualifies as a dimension of the 'poetized' (*das Gedichtete*), shall 'that peculiar domain containing the truth of the poem [. . .] be

---

97 Benjamin, 'Task of the Translator' in *SW*, VOL. 1, p. 260.

98 Benjamin, 'Two Poems by Friedrich Hölderlin' in *SW*, VOL. 1, pp. 18–36.

opened up.'[99] As we have seen, this is a conclusion that Benjamin will be able to discover in the theories of Schlegel and Novalis. It is decisive that Benjamin grasps, as the organ of these Romantic theorizations of the 'poetry of poetry', the notion of 'symbolic form',[100] and attributes to art criticism the task of representing 'this symbolic form in its purity.'[101]

In the opening of the work—which is guaranteed both by the delineation of its symbolic valence and by its taking root in the 'poetized'—a rhythmic correspondence comes to be created between these conditions, which articulate its dynamic, and that symbolic paradise of language that emerges in perfect examples of translation.

Hölderlin's translations of Sophocles, 'which date from that late period, which Hellingrath did not call the poet's "baroque" period for nothing,'[102] are the perfect archetype of translation, because his translations 'in particular are subject to the enormous danger inherent in all translations: the gates of a language thus expanded and modified may slam shut and enclose the translator in silence.' In the poet's anxiety to purify, 'meaning plunges from abyss to abyss until it threatens to become lost in the bottomless depths of language.'[103] But this limit-situation is entirely in keeping with the condition of the human species driven from Paradise. Benjamin did not hesitate to draw out the insecurities of translation, the always vacillating certainties of meaning, to a point of agony. The judging word, the profane word, must be thrown into jeopardy if one wants to preserve language at a juncture where being bursts in, interrogating it to discover its secret. The word of the translator must hold out, face to face with the hollows that continuously open up in the original, dedicated to the impossible and ever-renewing task of repeating in itself the origin, which is in this way sacralised.

---

99 Benjamin, 'Two Poems by Friedrich Hölderlin' in *SW*, VOL. 1, pp. 18–19.

100 Benjamin, 'Concept of Criticism in German Romanticism' in *SW*, VOL. 1, p. 171.

101 Benjamin, 'Concept of Criticism in German Romanticism' in *SW*, VOL. 1, p. 172.

102 Benjamin, *Origin of German Tragic Drama*, p. 189.

103 Benjamin, 'Task of the Translator' in *SW*, VOL. 1, p. 49.

4. Symbol: Tragic time and silence

Benjamin proposed the interlinear translation of the Bible as an archetype for all translation. But as always happens in a thought that feeds itself exclusively on the continuous reciprocal transfusion and inter-relation of its sources—in the echo created by an appropriately labyrinthine expositional structure—the appearance of this protean conclusion transforms itself immediately into the first move in a new game of speculation.

In a letter to Herbert Belmore dated approximately to the end of 1916, Benjamin announced—in a list of his writings—the completion, among other works, of the drafts of two essays: '*Trauerspiel* and Tragedy' and 'The Role of Language in *Trauerspiel* and Tragedy'.[104] These youthful texts attempt to determine the form of tragedy on the basis of its constitutional temporality, in relation to the differently oriented temporality of history. The spark for this comes, more radically, from a contrastive comparison of historical time and mechanical time, the latter of which is devised by the exact sciences of nature:

> Historical time is infinite in every direction and unfulfilled at every moment. This means we cannot conceive of a single empirical event that bears a necessary relation to the time of its occurrence. For empirical events time is nothing but a form, but, what is more important, as a form it is unfulfilled. The event does not fulfil the formal nature of the time in which it takes place. For we should not think of time as merely the measure that records the duration of a mechanical change. Although such time is indeed a relatively empty form, to think of its being filled makes no sense. Historical time, however, differs from this mechanical time [. . .] And without specifying what goes beyond this, what else determines historical time—in short, without defining how it differs from mechanical time—we may assert that the determining force of historical time

104 Benjamin, *Correspondence*, p. 84.

> cannot be fully grasped by, or wholly concentrated in, any empirical process.[105]

As we can see, in Benjamin the problem of the historicity of the living spirit takes on quite a particular valence, founded not on the recognition of 'existential' realms in the being of mankind, but in the paradoxical reversal—effected within Kantianism—of the empty formalism of an intuitive function into the richness of germinal determinations deriving from the refusal of the 'idea' to fix itself within the empirical. What should be stressed as crucial here is what is detailed, in terms of the concept of the historical form of time, within the term 'force'.

The repudiation of the time dear to the mechanical-causal sciences, devoid of quality and objectified in the irreversible repetition of the punctuality of events, does not aim, in Benjamin, to replace it—as is typical of any spiritualistic, merely apparently alternative, formulation—by time's insertion into the expanse of consciousness. The foundation of temporality takes place, instead, only thanks to its *historical* predicate. The plexus of time and historicity constitutes itself, in Benjamin, not as a result of the intentions, however similar, of an existential analytics, but through recourse to the notion of fulfilment (*Erfüllung*). Individual events do not unendingly fill up a time conceived as a 'void'. On the contrary, this time is laden with a latent nucleus so explosive as to require, potentially, the annihilation of any occurrence. In a manner entirely similar to the behaviour granted to history by the later notion of 'origin' in his book on the baroque, Benjamin here justifies historical time only in light of its non-historical, ultimate *Erfüllung* in the messianic state. In Benjamin, this messianic state has always seen its contours delineated more against the background of a prophetic eschatology than in the close-up view of a utopian perspective.[106] One result of this is

105 Benjamin, '*Trauerspiel* and Tragedy' in *SW*, VOL. 1, p. 55.

106 This is so at least according to this fundamental observation by Martin Buber: 'The vision of rightness in revelation is realized in the picture of a perfect *time*: as messianic eschatology. The vision of rightness in the ideal is realized in the picture of a perfect *space*: as Utopia.' *Paths in Utopia* (R. F. C. Hull trans.) (Boston: Beacon Press, 1958[1949]), p. 8.

Adorno's probable error in attributing the 'Theological-Political Fragment' to the final period of Benjamin's activity.[107] In this fragment, the image of historical time faithfully repeats what is given in the 1916 manuscript:

> Only the Messiah himself completes all history, in the sense that he alone redeems, completes, creates its relation to the messianic. For this reason, nothing that is historical [*Historisches*] can relate itself, from its own ground, to anything messianic. Therefore, the Kingdom of God is not the telos of the historical dynamic; it cannot be established as a goal.[108]

The historical nature of empirical events is messianic precisely due to the total fragility of their continuous passing, which is a promise of fulfilment—more than any voluntaristic striving towards a goal—already present in the pure concept of its ending.

> A process that is perfect in historical terms is quite indeterminate empirically; it is in fact an idea. This idea of fulfilled time is the dominant historical idea of the Bible: it is the idea of messianic time. Moreover, the idea of a fulfilled historical time is never identical with the idea of an individual time. This feature naturally changes the meaning of fulfilment [*Erfülltheit*] completely, and it is this that distinguishes tragic time from messianic time. Tragic time is related to the latter in the same way that an individually fulfilled time relates to a divinely fulfilled one.[109]

It would perhaps not be too much to say that the notion of 'tragic time' elaborated here is the exact equivalent of every cult of the theological symbol. The future separation of allegory from the 'auraticity' of the symbol[110] cannot, that is, take place except by first abandoning this

---

107 Adorno, *Über Walter Benjamin*, p. 29. In a note on p. 168 of Adorno's volume, Rolf Tiedemann points out that the fragment must have been written around 1920.

108 Benjamin, 'Theological-Political Fragment' in *SW*, VOL. 3, p. 305.

109 Benjamin, '*Trauerspiel* and Tragedy' in *SW*, VOL. 1, pp. 55–56.

110 This is the fitting term given by Adorno in his letter dated 18 March 1936 to Benjamin; see Adorno, *Über Walter Benjamin*, p. 127.

youthful theory of the tragic.[111] The individual fulfilment of divine time in the mundane historical realm always meets an inevitable defeat. How can the necessary failure of this willed striving reconcile itself with the idea of messianic time achieved? No messianic religion knows the form of tragedy. To the determination of tragic temporality, in the immobile ecstasy of an arbitrarily provoked contact with divine time, the decisive element remains concealed. In fact, the splendour of the messianic state may be looked at, without offense, not in the infinitely blinding reflection of an individual fulfilment, but in the opaque mirror of rhythmic temporal flow, in the humble guise of historical time.

> The spiritual *restitutio in integrum*, which introduces immortality, corresponds to a worldly [*weltliche*] restitution that leads to an eternity of downfall, and the rhythm of this eternally transient worldly existence, transient in its totality, in its spatial but also in its temporal totality, the rhythm of messianic nature, is happiness. For nature is messianic by reason of its eternal and total passing away [*Vergängnis*].[112]

This notion of happiness is decisive in Benjamin's thinking. It alone permits him, in fact, to overcome the mythical and pagan search for a tragic time as an 'auratic' moment of human redemption. The apparently humble proposal of 'One-Way Street'—'To be happy is to be able to

---

111 'In tragedy the hero dies because no one can live in unfulfilled time. He dies of immortality. Death is an ironic immortality; that is the origin of tragic irony. The origin of tragic guilt can be found in the same place. It has its roots in the tragic hero's very own, individually fulfilled time. This time of the tragic hero [. . .] describes all his deeds and his entire existence as if with a magic circle [. . .] It is almost a paradox that this becomes manifest in all its clarity at the moment when the hero is completely passive, when tragic time bursts open, so to speak, like a flower whose calyx emits the astringent perfume of irony. For it is not unusual for the fateful climax of the hero's time to reach its moment of fulfilment during moments of utter tranquility—during his sleep, as it were. And in the same way the meaning of the fulfilled time of a tragic fate emerges in the great moments of passivity: in the tragic decision, the retarding point of the action, and in the catastrophe.' Benjamin, '*Trauerspiel* and Tragedy' in *SW*, VOL. 1, p. 56.

112 Benjamin, 'Theological-Political Fragment' in *SW*, VOL. 3, pp. 305–6.

become aware of oneself without fright'[113]—requires the most radical critique of any conception of history as destiny. Human terror, in fact, lives in the 'magnetic field' of guilt in the same way that guilt dwells in the orbit of destiny.

> Happiness is, rather, what releases the fortunate man from the embroilment of the Fates and from the net of his own fate. Not for nothing does Hölderlin call the blissful gods 'fateless'. Happiness and bliss are therefore no more part of the sphere of fate than is innocence.[114]

The redemption promised by the blessed caducity of historical time is denied to the reawakening, however proud it may be, of tragic unhappiness. In fact, 'The guilt context is temporal in a totally inauthentic way, very different in its kind and measure from the time of redemption, or of music, or of truth.'[115] Tragic time is incapable of opening a horizon of freedom, an opening for hope in the fatal cycle that measures out the steps of what is 'not an autonomous time, but is parasitically dependent' on 'the time of a higher, less natural life.'[116] The order of destiny, in the absence of any reversal of guilt, knows no redemptive state. Even if tragic time concedes a liberating dimension, this does not shimmer in messianic light, but emerges confused in the wake of the laborious escape from myth. As the *Origin* will make definitively clear, the tragic hero who attempts to escape from the context of natural guilt can never redeem himself in the sense intended by Judaic messianism or Christian eschatology, precisely because in the sphere of fate, in contrast to any religious sphere, the condemnation is not the consequence of sin, but rather its condition. Tragedy uniquely reaches the point in which the dominion of this mythical brutality is broken. 'But not by having the endless pagan chain of guilt and atonement superseded by the purity of the man who

---

113 Benjamin, 'One-Way Street' in *SW*, VOL. 1, p. 463.

114 Benjamin, 'Fate and Character' in *SW*, VOL. 1, p. 203.

115 Benjamin, 'Fate and Character' in *SW*, VOL. 1, p. 204.

116 Benjamin, 'Fate and Character' in *SW*, VOL. 1, p. 204.

has expiated his sins, who is reconciled with the pure God.'[117] Tragic time can never know the fulfilment of this union because, as we have seen, it is not allowed to associate the moment of individual success with the idea of happiness. If we can therefore recognize a 'force' in historical time it is precisely that of knowing how to preserve, uncontaminated, the richness of this idea of the image of a fulfilment that is never just half-anticipated (which would be in vain) but is posited instead as the literal end of an inspired caducity of events. 'The fixation of one's own need and one's own longing mars the idea of a happiness that will not arise until the category of the individual ceases to be self-seclusive.'[118] The insufficiency of individual fulfilment, realizing itself in tragic time, thus requires, eschatologically, 'the idea of an objectivity of happiness, as Kierkegaard conceived it negatively in his doctrine of objective despair.'[119]

Since happiness is a completely historical category, unreachable by the sacrifice of the tragic hero, the result of tragedy can never be the demand for the redemption of historical time. More simply, through tragic poetry the mythical epoch comes to separate itself from a different temporal dimension that falls entirely within the setting of history. 'The signature of tragedy does not therefore consist in a "conflict of levels" between the hero and the environment as such, which is what Scheler declares to be characteristic in his study *Zum Phänomen des Tragischen*, but the unique Greek form of such conflicts.'[120] Thus it is necessary to clearly reject the characteristic tendency of the tragic to present itself, on the strength of its ostensible messianic character and the decisive resolution it appears to present, as a generically human and meta-historical category. The blunder Benjamin commits in 1916 of considering Christian *Trauerspiele* also to be tragedies has its authentic motive in the erroneous attribution of the *Erfüllung* to the tragic, which is thus led to claim for itself a value as a universal ethical category.

---

117 Benjamin, 'Fate and Character' in *SW*, VOL. 1, p. 203.

118 Adorno, *Negative Dialectics*, p. 352.

119 Adorno, *Negative Dialectics*, p. 353.

120 Benjamin, *The Origin of German Tragic Drama*, p. 106.

But the testimony that tragic time offers about the natural character of being fated to guilt constitutes uniquely 'the particular foundation of that more general understanding according to which the characters in a fiction can never be subject to ethical judgment.'[121] In the work's nocturnal character, there is no possibility for the *chiaroscuro* which is the essence of any moral judgment. As the essay 'Fate and Character' had asserted, the opposite, liberating vision of the natural innocence of men is seen in the comedy of character, without the least play of shadow and light, as though the tenebrous infernal strata had simply melted away. We could therefore say that it is the very inseparable connection of art and nature that discloses, 'the necessity of understanding the moral content of tragic poetry, not as its last word, but as one aspect of its integral truth: that is to say in terms of the philosophy of history.'[122] The occasionality of the liberating import of tragic time cannot be grasped in any other way than this.

The comprehensive explanation of Greek tragedy offered us by the *Origin* should not be read in the weak light reflected by its contingent polemic against any attempt to bring back to life, neoclassically, the schema of a form that is inexorably historical. Something else is at stake here, above all, the redemption of historical temporality but then, more radically (to return to the point we started from), the nexus of language and truth, whose bond, in the diverse guises of symbol or allegory, is assured by the different valences which the relation between time and history assumes in them.

The realm of the tragic seals itself up, Benjamin explains, in the surface of a triangular inter-relation. Its perimeter extends between the points constituted, at equal distance, by the idea of sacrifice, the agonistic schema, and the notion of silence. To begin with, Wilamowitz's hypothesis that tragedy draws its material from the saga must be qualified by the specification that such an inheritance is transformed into something qualitatively new. The quiet surface of the epic lake where the mythical

121 Benjamin, 'Goethe's *Elective Affinities*' in *SW*, vol. 1, p. 304.

122 Benjamin, *The Origin of German Tragic Drama*, p. 105 (translation modified).

patrimony of the saga placidly burbles, begins to ripple and then surge when the force of the tragic river bursts upon it. 'Tragic poetry is opposed to epic poetry as a tendentious re-shaping of the tradition.'[123] This deformation does not result, however, in a presumed poetics of the arbitrary, in the license of subjective invention: 'For the reshaping of the legend is not motivated by the search for tragic situations, but it is undertaken with a tendentious purpose which would lose all its significance if the tendency were not expressed in terms of the legend, the primordial history of the nation.'[124] The stigma of ambiguity brands the event that springs from this design with a link that can only be dissolved by a burning will. It imprints itself in the symbolic, enigmatic doubleness of the death of the victim, where,

> in respect of its victim, the hero, the tragic sacrifice differs from any other kind, being at once a first and a final sacrifice. A final sacrifice in the sense of the atoning sacrifice to gods who are upholding an ancient right; a first sacrifice in the sense of the representative action, in which new aspects of the life of the nation become manifest.[125]

The tragic dimension continues to remain entangled in the natural life of myth. Because if, on the one hand, tragic death tramples the ancient juridical authority of the Olympian gods, on the other it does nothing but offer up 'the hero to the unknown god as the first fruits of a new harvest of humanity.'[126] The dialecticity of this situation is so unresolvable that it cannot be fixed in the compact presence of reality. No physicality can incarnate this double meaning of death; its tension can be measured only in symbolic representation. It is precisely here that 'Death thereby becomes salvation.'[127] And in such a paradoxical state, tragic time is as though held back from the fulfilment of its trajectory in the magic circle

---

123 Benjamin, *The Origin of German Tragic Drama*, p. 106.

124 Benjamin, *The Origin of German Tragic Drama*, p. 106.

125 Benjamin, *The Origin of German Tragic Drama*, pp. 106–7.

126 Benjamin, *The Origin of German Tragic Drama*, p. 107.

127 Benjamin, *The Origin of German Tragic Drama*, p. 107.

of messianic time. In silence, in muteness, is smothered the tragic hero's cry of victory, which would break the mythical world's destiny of enchained guilt. Nothing but this can accurately define the tragic essence of the agonistic situation, that is, the failure of the community to accept the heroic word, isolating the rebel in his glacial pride, leaving him alone face to face with his promethean fury. In this way, 'the conclusion of a tragedy is still somehow removed from the sure triumph of the person-salvation-God principle [*menschheilgott-Prinzip*], and that even there a kind of *non liquet* lingers as an undertone.'[128] The prophetic voice of the hero is as though petrified by the inertia of the surrounding void which offers no echoing resistance:

> The greater the discrepancy between the tragic word and the situation—which can no longer be called tragic when there is no discrepancy—the more surely has the hero escaped the ancient statutes to which, when they finally overtake him, he throws only the dumb shadow of his being, the self, as a sacrifice, while his soul finds refuge in the word of a distant community.[129]

Suspended between myth and utopia, historical time cannot long survive in this paradoxical dimension. This 'paradox of the birth of genius in moral speechlessness, moral infantility,'[130] is indeed sublime. But the flight of this hope is brief, sporadic, and limited. After an instant of dismay, the indignant cry of the hero is reabsorbed into the mythical order of nature. 'The intoxicated, ecstatic word' of the hero is only the confession of defeat,[131] an act of flailing to delay the inevitable, the pretext thrown up to prolong the contest with the Olympians and slow the crucifixion of silence. Because the irruption of silence is what reveals tragic time as mythical in its attempt to block the cyclical return of the natural event.

---

128 Letter to Florence Christian Rang, 20 January 1924, in Benjamin, *Correspondence*, p. 231.

129 Benjamin, *The Origin of German Tragic Drama*, p. 109.

130 Benjamin, 'Fate and Character' in *SW*, VOL. 1, p. 203.

131 Benjamin, *The Origin of German Tragic Drama*, p. 116.

When, in taking up the question of allegory, Benjamin recalls its foundation in historicity, there is an implicit reference to the different configuration of temporality that flows from the relation between myth and tragedy. If tragedy has revealed itself, in its most extreme results, as the authentic 'myth of the failure of myth,'[132] an analogous failure is destined to break the promise of redemption and fulfilment, elevated from the symbol as representative of the ostensible messianism of tragic time. Only the symbol in its hieratic nakedness, its icy formality, seems to recognize the enchantment that fixes the tumult, the burst of tragic ecstasy, in that sublime moment that cleaves the impenetrable waters of silence. 'The measure of time for the experience of the symbol is the mystical instant in which the symbol assumes the meaning into its hidden and, if one might say so, wooded interior.'[133] This mystical instant thus stands as the exact equivalent of the instantaneousness of the redemption invoked by the individual time of tragedy. While in the allegory of the baroque *Trauerspiele*, 'the observer is confronted with the *facies hippocratica* of history as a petrified, primordial landscape,' it is only in the symbol that 'the transfigured face of nature is fleetingly revealed in the light of redemption.'[134] The auratic character of the symbol thus knows only perfect unity, without detritus, with the other-than-self, with the sphere of significance that the symbol intends.

We might here characterize with a formula the space where the collapse of tragic time and the proud muteness of the hero cross paths. It is precisely their symbolic nature that misses the moment of redemption. If the messianic state allows itself to be known only in the prophetic word, this cannot bear to be touched even in the slightest degree by the suspicion of expressing anything other than reality in its pure state. In prophecy, everything must be taken literally.

---

132 Roland Barthes, *On Racine* (Richard Howard trans.) (New York: Performing Arts Journal Publications, 1983), p. 60.

133 Benjamin, *The Origin of German Tragic Drama*, p. 165.

134 Benjamin, *The Origin of German Tragic Drama*, p. 166.

CHAPTER THREE

The Problem of History

1. Walter Benjamin's *Passagenwerk*

With the publication of *Passagenwerk* (*The Arcades Project*) in 1982,[1] the different directions taken by all of Benjamin's production subsequent to the great book on German Baroque Drama—which had appeared in the form of brief and rhapsodic interventions in mostly contingent contexts closely bound to the socio-historical circumstances of the 1930s—now finally recompose themselves as individual tiles in a single precious mosaic. As it presents itself to us today in its state of ruin, like a boundless field of construction materials, the *Arcades Project* is a rediscovered Pompeii whose villas of the mysteries we can now finally try to interpret. Independently of the recent, unverifiable conjectures about the disappearance of a supposedly definitive draft of the work after Benjamin's last, tragic flight across the Pyrenees,[2] we must seek to reconstruct the final lineaments of his philosophy on the basis of the current version, whose 'unfinished' state is probably original to and constitutive of the meaning of the work itself.[3] In view of the current status of the edition of the *Arcades*, then, the problem seems rather that of understanding why the primitive nucleus of a work whose general theoretical profile was basically already fully delineated in the barely fifty pages of its first version of 1927,[4] only gave rise—after an extremely laborious process of

1 Walter Benjamin, *Das Passagen-Werk* (Rolf Tiedemann ed.), *Gesammelte Schriften*, VOL. 5, 2 PARTS (Frankfurt am Main: Surhkhamp, 1982). First published in English translation as *The Arcades Project* (Howard Eiland and Kevin McLaughlin trans, Rolf Tiedmann ed.) (Cambridge, MA: Belknap Press, 2002).

2 See Lisa Fittko, 'The Story of Old Benjamin' in Benjamin, *Arcades Project*, pp. 946–54.

3 See the observations by Rolf Tiedemann in the notes to 'Zeugnisse zur Ensthungsgeschichte' in *Passagen-Werk*, pp. 1183–205.

4 See Benjamin, 'First Sketches' in *Arcades Project*, pp. 827–68.

rethinking and adjustment—as its only truly novel theoretical result, to the brief theses 'On the Concept of History', otherwise scattering itself in an infinite—over a thousand pages—meander of *Aufzeichnungen* (notes), where the theoretical flow is constructed from the accumulated detritus of the citations. In such a context, the theses of 'On the Concept of History' (which, having been assigned by the plan of the edition to the volume of the *Abhandlungen* [treatises], were paradoxically torn from their original destination)[5] end up configuring themselves into a sort of reappropriation of the most vital theoretical nucleus contained in the *Urpassagen* drafted at the end of the 1920s. Benjamin undertook the materialistic reformulation of this nucleus in response to requests coming from the Institute for Social Research, which had agreed to sponsor the work. The reformulation was supposed to be at the same time a rewriting of the enigmatic language of the *Denkbilder* (thought-images)—which is ultimately what the *Urpassagen* are—into a soberly conceptual language, but such a rewriting never took place. In the overall economy of the *Passagenwerk* as it has come down to us in the current edition, the *Urpassagen* seem literally to constitute for Benjamin a rigorously safeguarded *treasure box* to which he might always return, however parsimoniously, to embellish and bring to a shine the otherwise unshowy texture of the citations and the purely bibliographical material.

What then is the philosophy that inspires the aphorisms of the *Urpassagen*? In a brief approximation, it could be defined as a *metacriticism of surrealism*. Surrealism, the philosophy of intoxication, of metropolitan shock, must subject itself in turn to a salutary jolt: one constituted by the 'ultra-intoxication' of reason. Similar to the image of the Zuyder Zee in Freud,[6] what arises in Benjamin in his encounter with the Surrealists is the idea of a work of reclamation of reason.

---

5 See Benjamin, 'On the Concept of History' in *SW*, VOL. 4, pp. 389–400.

6 'Where id was, there ego shall be. It is reclamation work, like the draning of the Zuyder Zee.' The Zuyder Zee (also Zuider Zee, or Zuyderzee) was a shallow bay in the Netherlands' North Sea, which was reclaimed as land by the building of the Afsluitdijk dam, between 1927 and 1932. See Sigmund Freud, *New Introductory Lectures on Psycho-Analysis* (New York: Carlton House, 1933), p. 112. [Trans.]

> To cultivate fields where, until now, only madness has reigned. Forge ahead with the whetted axe of reason, looking neither right nor left so as not to succumb to the horror that beckons from deep in the primeval forest. But every ground must at some point have been turned over by reason, must have been cleared of the undergrowth of delusion and myth. This is to be accomplished here for the terrain of the nineteenth century.[7]

Against the surrealist philosophy of the dream, Benjamin has, with innumerable variations, countered with a doctrine of 'awakening'. 'Delimitation of the tendency of this project with respect to Aragon: whereas Aragon persists within the realm of dream, here the concern is to find the constellation of awakening.'[8] What does this contraposition really consist of? Benjamin grants to the Surrealists—Aragon above all—the essential merit of having deciphered the originally archaic character of modernity, now interpreted as myth. Speaking of a 'primal history of the nineteenth century',

> would be of no interest if it were understood to mean that forms of primal history are to be recovered among the inventory of the nineteenth century. Only where the nineteenth century would be presented as originary form of primal history—as a form, that is to say, in which the *whole* of primal history so renews itself that certain of its older traits would be recognized only as precursors of these recent ones—only there does this concept of a primal history of the nineteenth century have meaning.[9]

Benjamin reproaches surrealism, however, for having remained prisoner of the same phantasmagoria that it brings into evidence. In *Le Paysan*

7 Benjamin, 'First Sketches' in *Arcades Project*, p. 842.

8 Benjamin, 'First Sketches' in *Arcades Project*, p. 845.

9 Benjamin, 'First Sketches' in *Arcades Project*, p. 864; see also Walter Benjamin, 'N. On the Theory of Knowledge, Theory of Progress' in 'Convolutes', *Arcades Project*, p. 463 [N3a,2].

de Paris, Aragon—it's true—recognized the irremediably antiquated character of the *passage*, its prehistoric configuration, but he was unable to free himself from the oneiric reproposition of this same past. What is important above all are the ways the *Urpassagen* circumscribe the modes of this 'awakening' from the surrealist dream. Awakening is a 'technique' of departure from the past, the occasion for an overturning which, in order to succeed, requires 'cunning'. 'The genuine liberation from an epoch, that is, has the structure of awakening in this respect as well: it is entirely ruled by cunning. Only with cunning, not without it, can we work free of the realm of dream.' The model of cunning counters that of 'a false liberation; its sign is violence.' 'Of course, in the end, the law according to which an action brings about an opposite reaction holds true [. . .] From the beginning, it condemned *Jugendstil* to failure.'[10] In the undertaking to separate the awakening from any kind of 'false redemption,'[11] Benjamin has arrived at a point where he can descry the ultimate model in 'dialectics': 'There is a wholly unique experience [*Erfahrung*] of dialectic. The compelling—the drastic—experience, which refutes everything "gradual" about becoming and shows all seeming "development" to be dialectical reversal, eminently and thoroughly composed, is the awakening from dream.'[12] What is this 'cunning' in dialectics that, as a genuine awakening, must know how to distinguish itself from the false liberation of 'violence'? Borrowing from the young Marx's September 1843 letter to Runge, in the epistemological notes on the notion of progress that constitute the immediate precursor to the final theses 'On the Concept of History', Benjamin emphasized the quality of 'gaiety' which the dialectical overturning must have. Once again, the archetype of this gaiety is Surrealism, because, 'Surrealism is the death of the nineteenth century in comedy.'[13] 'A reconciled humanity will take

10 Walter Benjamin, 'G. Exhibitions, Advertising, Grandville' in *Arcades Project*, p. 172–73. ['Frühe Entwürfe' in *Passagen-Werk*, p. 1058.]

11 Walter Benjamin, 'Materials for the Exposé of 1935' in *Arcades Project*, p. 908.

12 Benjamin, 'First Sketches' in *Arcades Project*, p. 838.

13 Benjamin, 'On the Theory of Knowledge, Theory of Progress' in *Arcades Project*, p. 467.

leave of its past—and one form of reconciliation is gaiety.'[14] In awakening, the *Umschlag* (reversal) can be achieved only if the leave-taking from the oneiric world of phantasmagoria, from that genuine 'hell' ('Modernity; the time of hell')[15] which is the mythological world of modernity, is not simply a liquidation, but rather a rising up into consciousness. This is why in such a context Benjamin reappropriates Marx's famous statement:

> Our election cry must be: Reform of consciousness not through dogmas but through the analysis of mystical consciousness that is unclear to itself [. . .] Then people will see that the world has long possessed the dream of a thing—and that it only needs to possess the consciousness of this thing in order really to possess it.[16]

From this perspective, the most precise and detailed formulation that Benjamin furnished of his embryonic doctrine of awakening is that which makes awakening itself,

> the great exemplar of memory—that occasion on which we succeed in remembering what is nearest, most obvious (in the 'I'). What Proust intends with the experimental rearrangement of furniture, what Bloch recognizes as the darkness of the lived moment, is nothing other than what here is secured on the level of the historical, and collectively. There is a not-yet-conscious knowledge of *what has been*: its advancement has the structure of awakening.[17]

What is the relation, then, between awakening and remembering? Furthermore, what is the nexus between the critique of progress—which encapsulates the historical-philosophical meaning of Benjamin's work

---

14 Benjamin, 'On the Theory of Knowledge, Theory of Progress' in *Arcades Project*, p. 467.

15 Benjamin, 'First Sketches' in *Arcades Project*, p. 842.

16 Benjamin, 'On the Theory of Knowledge, Theory of Progress' in *Arcades Project*, p. 467.

17 Walter Benjamin, 'The Arcades of Paris' in 'Early Drafts', *Arcades Project*, p. 883.

on the *passages* from an epistemological perspective—and the theory of awakening as remembering? In the theory of awakening there is at work something Benjamin defines as a 'dialectical schematism', in which only memory can constitute the true point of conversion from dream to awakening:[18]

> Dialectical structure of awakening: remembering and awaking are most intimately related. Awakening is namely the dialectical, Copernican turn of remembrance [*Eingedenken*]. It is an eminently composed reversal from the world of dreaming to the world of waking. For the dialectical schematism at the core of this physiological process, the Chinese have found, in their fairy tales and novellas, the most radical expression. The new, dialectical method of doing history teaches us to pass in spirit—with the rapidity and intensity of dreams—through what has been, in order to experience the present as waking world, a world to which every dream at last refers.[19]

In such a schema, memory is understood in light of the concept of 'threshold' (*Schwelle*) which, in these same pages, Benjamin insistently opposes to that of *Grenze*, that is, limit or border: 'Threshold and boundary must be very carefully distinguished. The *Schwelle* is a zone. And indeed a zone of transition.'[20] Awakening is not a caesura with the world of dreams, not a hiatus with the world of the past—which Marx himself rejects in the quoted letter to Ruge. It is, rather, the redemption of that same world of dream, or more exactly its passage into a region Benjamin defines as the region of 'recognizability':

> Is awakening perhaps the synthesis of dream consciousness (as thesis) and waking consciousness (as antithesis)? Then the moment of awakening would be identical with the 'now of recognizability' in which things put on their true—Surrealist—

18 Benjamin, 'The Arcades of Paris' in *Arcades Project*, p. 884.

19 Benjamin, 'The Arcades of Paris' in *Arcades Project*, p. 884.

20 Benjamin, 'First Sketches' in *Arcades Project*, p. 856.

> face. Thus, in Proust, the importance of staking an entire life on life's supremely dialectical point of rupture: awakening. Proust begins with an evocation of the space of someone waking up.[21]

It is important to dwell on this metaphor of the threshold, in its diverse variations, as the best indicator to bring us close to conceiving of awakening-memory. Awakening is a point of fluctuation, of transition: Only in memory is it capable of finding the material of consciousness. In accomplishing its function as a critical threshold, awakening, on the one hand, acts as a meta-criticism of surrealist mythology, turning to recognize that 'the now (is) the inmost image of what has been.'[22] At the same time, in its commemorative essence, it disenchants the most profound dream of the nineteenth century, that dream of progress which transmigrated from bourgeois ideology into the very heart of vulgar Marxism. For Benjamin, the dream without awakening of the Surrealists is nothing but the other face of awakening without a dream, awakening as *Grenze*, as hiatus, which is co-essential to the acritical philosophy of progress; that philosophy, that is, in which progress 'becomes the signature of historical process *as a whole*.'[23]

But how is this theory of awakening as memory compatible with the revolutionary messianism latent in the concluding theses of 'On the Concept of History', which formally and thematically fit in every aspect with the philosophical perspective of the *Arcades Project*? In other words, doesn't the rupture with the empty time of history inaugurated by modernity—this '*monde dominé par ses fantasmagories*' (world dominated by its phantasmagorias)[24]—seem precisely to imply a concept of awakening as limit rather than threshold, or as hiatus rather than passage?

---

21 Benjamin, 'On the Theory of Knowledge, Theory of Progress' in *Arcades Project*, p. 464.

22 Benjamin, 'First Sketches' in *Arcades Project*, p. 865.

23 Benjamin, 'On the Theory of Knowledge, Theory of Progress' in *Arcades Project*, p. 478.

24 Walter Benjamin, 'Exposé of 1939' in *Arcades Project*, p. 26.

And lastly, what are we to make of the critique of the social-democratic distortions of Marx's theory, which powers the most polemical pages of the theses? It is a question here of the most subtle point in Benjamin's historico-philosophical conception, which risks being completely misunderstood. But only in this way can we hope to understand why Benjamin affirms that 'awakening from the dream' constitutes 'an absolutely unique experience of dialectics.' His dialectics consists in this, that in Benjamin the critique of myth and its rescue are absolutely simultaneous: without awakening, neither would there be any experience of the dream, just as, vice versa, without the dream it would be impossible to perceive the absolute novelty of awakening. Benjamin's efforts are wholly focused on creating an experience of, and giving a name to, the threshold that alone provides for the establishment of this dialectic between dream and waking, which is, precisely, memory. Just as the disenchantment of the dream is made out of love for the dream itself, in the same way, the critique of the past is not made in the name of an undefinable future, but rather in order to rescue caducity from its own destiny:

> Historical knowledge of the truth is possible only as overcoming the illusory appearance [*Aufhebung des Scheins*]. Yet this overcoming should not signify sublimation, actualization of the object, but rather assume, for its part, the configuration of a rapid image. The small quick figure in contrast to scientific complacency. This configuration of a *rapid* image goes together with the recognition of the 'now' in things. But not the future. Surrealist mien of things in the now; philistine mien in the future. The illusion overcome here is that an earlier time is in the now. In truth: the now 'is' the inmost image of what has been.[25]

In this sense, one may say that the entire project of the *Passagenwerk* is perhaps already contained in a marginal note to the description of the Passage l'Opéra in Aragon's *Paysan de Paris*. What is here 'at the centre

25 Benjamin, 'First Sketches' in *Arcades Project*, pp. 864–65.

of these questions', Benjamin writes, is a singular fact: 'the arcades are what they are for us here through the fact that they no longer are (in themselves).'[26] It is therefore the experience of the 'death of the Paris arcades',[27] that is the experience of the untruth of modernity's promise of the new, which drives Benjamin, despite everything, to attempt a rescue in the appearance of memory. The theses 'On the Concept of History' are thus only the transposition into the field of the philosophy of history of this same experience of the threshold-memory. Just as the awakening is the threshold which, opening up the difference between dream and waking, rescues the dream from the oblivion of its own unconsciousness, in the same way 'the image of redemption' can redeem the present only by awaking 'a not-yet-conscious knowledge of what has been.'[28] If waking is a threshold, in the same way, 'our life is a muscle strong enough to contract the whole of historical time.'[29]

2. Aesthetic time and historical time

It is striking to note in the theses 'On the Concept of History' how, every time he comes close to defining the concept of messianic time, Benjamin characterizes it, variously and repeatedly, by resorting to aesthetic terminology. Time after time, even in preparatory sketches and drafts, the effort at definition turns to Focillon's notion of 'classical style',[30] or insists

---

26 Benjamin, 'Materials for the Exposé of 1935' in *Arcades Project*, p. 909.

27 Benjamin, 'Materials for the Exposé of 1935' in *Arcades Project*, p. 909.

28 Benjamin, 'The Arcades of Paris' in *Arcades Project*, p. 883.

29 Benjamin, 'On the Theory of Knowledge, Theory of Progress' in *Arcades Project*, p. 479.

30 Benjamin, *Gesammelte Schriften*, VOL. 1, TOME 3, p. 1229: 'Classicism: a brief, perfectly balanced instant of complete possession of forms [. . .] a pure, quick delight, like the ἀκμή of the Greeks, so delicate that the pointer of the scale scarcely trembles. I look at this scale not to see whether the pointer will presently dip down again, or even come to a moment of absolute rest. I look at it instead to see, within the miracle of that hesitant immobility, the slight, inappreciable tremor that indicates life.' Henri Focillon, *The Life of Forms in Art* (George Kubler trans.) (Cambridge, MA: Zone Books, 1992), p. 55.

on the idea of prose.[31] But more often—and this is ultimately the preferred determination—Benjamin applies the concept of the image (*Bild*).[32] It is above all in the image that we must seek the key to open up the concept of historical time in Benjamin. This is the line that simultaneously connects and distinguishes the two decisive moments of his development, that is, the early period up to *The Origin of German Tragic Drama* and the mature period of the 1930s, marked approximately by his encounter with the theory of the proletariat. From the writings beginning in 1916 that contain in sketch form the strategic ideas of the great book on the *Ursprung*,[33] the aesthetic interpretation of the idea of redemption is a given, taking the form of an ideal of pure language, without judgement, whose paradigm is music. From this point of view, the sole genuine novelty is the disavowal which, by introducing the notion of *Bild*, the 1940 text enacts against the prohibition declared in the 'Epistemo-Critical Prologue' concerning the attempt of the 'adepts of all the theories of neo-Platonic paganism'[34] to interpret the idea not as word, but as vision, intuition. 'The being of ideas as they have been defined as components of truth,' Benjamin wrote in the first version of this prologue, 'absolutely cannot be thought of as endowed with the character of image [*als Bildhaftes*]. It cannot be arrived at through any intuition. Not even an intellectual one.'[35]

Besides this difference, at first glance essential, between a definition of the idea of redemption in terms of language versus one in terms of image, the 1940 theses still constitute, in substance, a reformulation of the judgement already pronounced about historical time as time of the *Trauerspiel*. Like the *Ursprung*, historical time is also a force field, once again the space of the salvation of phenomena as above all the salvation

31 Benjamin, 'Paralipomena to "On the Concept of History"' in *SW*, VOL. 4, p. 404.

32 Benjamin, 'On the Concept of History' in *SW*, VOL. 4, pp. 390–91.

33 Benjamin, '*Trauerspiel* and Tragedy' in *SW*, VOL. 1, pp. 55–74. These are '*Trauerspiel* and Tragedy', 'The Role of Language in *Trauerspiel* and Tragedy' and 'On Language as Such and On the Language of Man'.

34 Benjamin, *Origin of German Tragic Drama*, p. 35.

35 Benjamin, *Gesammelte Schriften*, VOL. 1, TOME 2, p. 936.

of the past. This past is the time of humanity whose memory [*ricordo*] one wishes to erase forever, to the benefit of the triumphal march towards the future of the conquering spirit. Historical time is only the articulation of this memory of the past, and this memory is in turn nothing more than an involuntary image: 'The dialectical image can be defined as the involuntary memory of redeemed humanity.'[36] It is decisive that the image within which memory takes shape and historical temporality assumes its dimensionality is determined not by a consciousness and an intentionality, but by involuntary reminiscence. The image rehabilitates itself by withdrawing from the arbitrary nature of conscious spirituality, fleeing the condemnation that the prologue to the *Origin* had declared towards its intuitive-intentional status. Just as the *Ursprung* was the space of the mediation and salvation of phenomena in the pure linguistic being of the idea, now, in the 1940 theses, historical time is the distension and articulation of the aesthetic time of the image. What is aesthetic time as the time of the image, properly speaking? The *Origin* had already furnished the decisive elements of an answer. Referencing Plato's *Symposium*, Benjamin had worked out the possibility of perceiving the linguistic being of ideas exclusively through the recognition of the constitutional nexus between truth and beauty. It is in beauty as appearance that the specific temporality of the soul is established, which eros drives towards the contemplation of the idea. Aesthetic temporality, as temporality of the soul, defines itself as the space of anamnesis. Finding the symbolic character of the word in which the idea reaches its own *Selbstverständigung* (self-understanding) can only be achieved, Benjamin writes, 'by recalling in memory the primordial form of perception. Platonic anamnesis is, perhaps, not far removed from this kind of remembering; except that here it is not a question of the actualization of images in visual terms.'[37] Only as an involuntary image can it become the go-between in an anamnesis, the field of mediation between memory and redemption. From this perspective, one can radically assert that, for

---

36 Benjamin, 'Paralipomena to "On the Concept of History"' in *SW*, VOL. 4, p. 403.

37 Benjamin, *The Origin of German Tragic Drama*, pp. 36–37.

Benjamin, aesthetic temporality, as temporality of the soul absorbed in the contemplation of the nexus of truth and beauty, is the very origin of temporality's self-offering, of temporality *tout court* as the space of memory. The salvation of appearance and the dimension of memory are all one: here is rooted the connection between temporality and the aesthetic dimension. The appearance constitutive of the space of redemption, and the beauty whose sacrifice would sacrifice the space of truth itself, are nothing other than memory continuously rescuing them from death in the space of historical time. It is precisely this connection, between the sphere of appearance as the sphere of irremediable caducity, and the counter-movement of memory in the involuntary image, that forms the nexus that some of the theses' most subtle passages struggle to delineate as the world of the soul, or rather the world of the past. The contiguity of appearance and memory that constitutes the originary nature of aesthetic time is that secret dwelling especially in metaphors like those of the breath (*Hauch*) or the echo: 'The past carries with it a secret index by which it is referred to redemption. Doesn't a breath of the air [*Hauch*] that pervaded earlier days caress us as well? In the voices we hear, isn't there an echo of now silent ones?'[38] And again, a variant of the fifth thesis reads:

> The past can be seized only as an image that flashes up at the moment of its recognizability, and is never seen again. It owes its authenticity to its fugacity. In this resides its only *chance*. Exactly because this truth is fleeting and borne to us on a breath [*Hauch*], much depends on it.[39]

In the theses of 'On the Concept of History', historical time is a mode of temporality that opens out of aesthetic time: this is the mobile space of the soul which, seeking to slow down appearance and fleeting caducity, manifests itself above all in the rescue of the past, in memory. The articulation of historical time entirely and only in the commemorative movement of the soul takes shape in Benjamin as a conscious attempt to slow

---

38 Benjamin, 'On the Concept of History' in *SW*, VOL. 4, p. 390.

39 Benjamin, 'On the Concept of History' in *SW*, VOL. 4, p. 390.

the haemorrhaging flight of time away from the space of memory, which is its characteristic sign in Christian-bourgeois modernity. The acceleration of history, beginning in the Enlightenment in the rupture with tradition and the configuration of a possible single, universal history that would unify event and representation—gathering up and directing all the heretofore scattered spiritual energies of humanity towards a future conceived as progress—is the reverse of the idea of historical time as Benjamin proposed it in the theses. What Koselleck, in relation to the specific temporality of the modern, defined as a 'temporalization of history' (*Verzeitlichung der Geschichte*),[40] would be determined, from Benjamin's perspective as considered here, as an exteriorization, an objectification of that movement of the soul that saves the past in the image. The modern temporalization of history is, for Benjamin, precisely that attempt to affirm truth without appearance, to render irrevocable the past by erasing its memory, and to affirm the future as the continuation of present happening, against which stands the movement the dialectical image. The dialecticity of this is, furthermore, a response to the paradoxicality, the ambivalence, of the phenomenon of *Verzeitlichung* (temporalization). Because this latter, as the spirit of modernity, is above all that movement with which the calculating *ratio* proceeds, as Simmel wrote in *The Philosophy of Money*, to the *Entseelung* (loss of soul) of the world, thus to the abolition, together with tradition, also of the faculty of memory as a particular gift of the soul. At the same time, it is equally that which, by breaking the empty continuum of tradition, making *tabula rasa* of the past, opens the space of discontinuity in which is solely possible the recuperation of other images of the past, beyond those handed down by tradition itself. The dialectical image is the attempt to reply to this paradoxicality with something of a superior order; it could be defined as the effort to re-interiorize temporalized history as memory, a history that, paradoxically, is the only one able to lead the soul to reawaken itself. Because the possibility of recourse opens up, surprisingly, exactly where history proceeds to cancel the past. The soul

40 See the essays in Reinhart Koselleck, *Futures Past: On the Semantics of Historical Time* (Keith Tribe trans.) (New York: Columbia University Press, 2004).

does not awaken to interiority except where the soul has extirpated the very last worldly trace of it. This is the decisive point of the history of the image, in Benjamin, as the primacy of aesthetic temporality, its character simultaneously dialectical and involuntary. This means that the commemorative force of the soul can establish itself only in the absence and loss resulting from the historical acceleration of time that attaches to the past the emblem of irrevocability: 'For it is an irretrievable image of the past which threatens to disappear in any present that does not recognize itself as intended in that image.'[41] The temporalization of history, which is simultaneously its *Entseelung* and the process of its uninterrupted rational spiritualization, is the event in which only the soul can become conscious of itself as soul, custodian of the memory of the past, protector of the kingdom of the dead and the defeated. In the movement of memory, temporalized history is that which becomes in turn appearance; this happens when the dialectical image endeavours to decipher history's intimate essence. What is, properly speaking, the temporalized history of modernity? It is the attempt to seize control in exteriority—as a *continuum* of temporal unfolding—of that intermittent, 'flashing',[42] discontinuous awareness of the irrevocability of the past held firm by the image-memory. Temporalized history is, in a certain sense, the objectification of this caducity, or rather the bourgeois attempt to appropriate it and, having done so, to eliminate it. Temporalized history is the objectification of the fleetingness and ephemerality in the new of a *continuum* in a state of perpetual becoming. The past, in its continuously repeated irrevocability, is the essence of modern spiritual history.

This caducity of the new is the appearance that objectifies itself, rendering itself available and instrumental, in the technical. The vindication of aesthetic time in the image against the temporalization of history in the modern is also born in Benjamin from the awareness that this latter is nothing but a counterfeit of originary time, that of the soul

---

41 Benjamin, 'On the Concept of History' in *SW*, VOL. 4, p. 391.

42 Benjamin, 'On the Concept of History' in *SW*, VOL. 4, pp. 390–91.

evoking appearance. Here is rooted also the meaning of the spasmodic attention that Benjamin dedicated to modernity as a phenomenon which is above all aesthetic. This attention harbours the awareness that the essence of modern historical time may be deciphered not in the ambivalent, instrumental project of the technical, but rather only in art as a conscious artificial construction of caducity, as a true elevation of appearance to essence. This demonstrates, furthermore, the partiality of recent readings of the 1936 essay on the technical reproducibility of the work of art. In fact, what is really at stake here is not the objectification of the aura and of artistic appearance in the technical universe, but, on the contrary, the unveiling of how the technical reveals, in no matter how contorted and mystified a form, the very essence of art; an essence which in the world of tradition could not help but remain concealed. Making the essential transitory, fixing the irrevocable: this is the secret of aesthetic time—a realm of memory and appearance—which in counterfeit form conceals itself also in the modern temporalization of history. In this last, however, the recognition of caducity and its objectification in the technical are placed at the service of the appropriative aim of the subject; the ephemeral is recognized and objectified, posited as past, but a past whose very purpose is always to be forgotten.

Thus, from the shadow of the reciprocal camouflaging in which art and the technical seem to be bound together in the modern, Benjamin shows us a glimmer of light, a delicate shading, in which all the ineliminable distance separating aesthetic time from historical time stands out. In fact, that past which, being ephemeral, is nothingness itself to historical time, is everything for aesthetic time, the very essence of truth.

As time of redemption, time of involuntary anamnesis, aesthetic time is that which, bringing to a halt the accelerated time of the modern, guides it instead to its originary self-awareness. The same *Verzeitlichung* of history in the modern, as discontinuity and rupture with tradition, is in fact born from the possibility to liberate a memory, to fix an appearance which seemed lost once and for all:

> Thus, to Robespierre ancient Rome was a past charged with now-time [*Jetztzeit*], a past which he blasted out of the continuum of history. The French Revolution viewed itself as Rome reincarnate. It cited ancient Rome exactly the way fashion cites a bygone mode of dress. Fashion has a nose for the topical, no matter where it stirs in the thickets of long ago; it is the tiger's leap into the past.[43]

This is the paradox inscribed in the dialecticity of the aesthetic image loaded with messianic time: once again, it is aesthetic consciousness—that movement of the soul that has led to the integral temporalization of history—that now must revoke the autonomization of this temporalization, which has objectified and exteriorized that movement into a nihilism of the spirit. In Benjamin, messianic time—the time of music, of the linguistic idea or the involuntary image—is the counter-movement that breaks the enchantment of this exteriorized history. It is not a matter of the absurd effort of abrogating the temporalization of history. Rather it is a question of establishing itself in the heart of this temporalization, of curving it around itself, restoring to it the memorial power of the origin. The aesthetic terms that Benjamin adopts to define the idea of messianic time should not therefore be considered, from this perspective, as mere metaphors. In aesthetic time as well as in the time of the saving of appearance, there is also in play the possibility of the rescue of 'true' history. Historical time can become original once again, as 'that which emerges from the process of becoming and disappearance,'[44] saved from losing its way in a blind temporal *continuum*—but only for the memory that knows how to save it anew as mere appearance, as irrevocable past, in the image. The time of redemption is a re-interiorization of historical time, folding in upon itself as though frozen in the crystallization of the image, of temporalization.

43 Benjamin, 'On the Concept of History' in *SW*, VOL. 4, p. 395.

44 Benjamin, *Origin of German Tragic Drama*, p. 45.

Having spent itself in memory, historical time again becomes that appearance which alone allows for truth to take on definition. Truth is revealed only in history as appearance, in the ever-repeating attempt to hold back the irrevocable, an attempt that delimits the anamnestic space of the soul. It is decisive, therefore, that this aesthetic time as time of the soul finds in history—finally led back to appearance—the space where the past can be saved. Only from the space of temporalized history, and only from the time of the spirit, can arise the true consciousness of appearance and, more radically, the very idea of a messianic time. Otherwise, the aesthetic temporality whose primacy Benjamin affirmed would collapse entirely into the space of myth, to become at most evocation, but it could never have the strength to constitute itself messianically in relation to history. In this regard, we may recall the distinction made by a youthful Benjamin in 1916[45] between tragic and historical time, or rather, as we could say, the time of the *Trauerspiel*: only in relation to the latter may arise the possibility of conceiving of redemption and the idea of a messianic time. Only in the space of history, which is also the space of revelation, can we posit the separation between truth and appearance and, thus, also the problem of the salvation (redemption) of appearance. In the confusion of myth, instead, phenomena clinging to what the *Origin* calls their false unity[46]—prior to conceptual articulations and divisions, and also prior to that, 'birth from becoming' which is history as origin—just as they are not aware of their character as appearance, neither can they rescue themselves in truth. Only temporalized history, as awareness of the irremediable caducity of the phenomenal, in the negation that constitutes the phenomenal nihilistically as essence, opens at the same time the space of that memory [*ricordo*] which will always keep hold of its appearance.

---

45 Benjamin, '*Trauerspiel* and Tragedy' in *SW*, VOL. 1, p. 55ff.

46 Benjamin, *Origin of German Tragic Drama*, p. 33.

CHAPTER FOUR

Conclusion: Towards a Philosophy of the Informal

An apparent unresolvability, a state of suspense, has been noted with regard to the discussion of aesthetics in Benjamin's dissertation on the concept of *Kunstkritik* in German proto-romanticism. The romantic aspiration towards a completely fulfilled, perfect mediation granted to the idea of form—conceived as self-reflection leading to an elevation in the power of the artwork through criticism—is counterposed to the Goethean ideal of the archetypal character of the content of art. Now, we would fail clearly to identify Benjamin's thinking were we to deem this tension to be paradigmatic and exemplary of the entire course of his work—an ambiguity, an undecided oscillation due to theoretical immaturity. Rather, starting from this same early tension around the idea of the artwork, it becomes possible to demonstrate that it is a constituent law of Benjamin's thought to situate himself, Goethe-like, in a polarity of extremes without trying to mediate them, but also without remaining in a position that can be called ambiguous or uncertain. The tension between idea and ideal of the artwork which closes his *Doktorarbeit* (doctoral dissertation) is the first demonstration of a motif that is the very nucleus of this experience of thought. The figure inaugurated by the tension between idea and ideal is typical and recognizable in the central passages of Benjamin's philosophy. In all his decisive moments, the scene of this thought situates at one pole a dimension of immanence, a field of dialectic mediations incapable of resolution, trapped in the nexus of guilt-destiny (world of myth, tragedy, bad romantic infinity, infernal modernity). At the other pole sits the heterological dimensions of that which has the capacity to flow away, to escape from this connection of immanence: the idea of the discontinuous, of verticality, of redemption (music, allegory, *Trauerspiel*, now-time). Thus, it is in the heterological moment, in what breaks the connection of immanence, that Benjamin believes we may find the dream of originary unity that precedes the polarity of the same and the other, of immanence and transcendence;[1] a unity prefigured in the irruption of transcendence. As in Kraus, in Benjamin too the origin is the goal, but the origin is given precisely in what discards and disarticulates the false mediations of the world after original sin. It is in the breakdown of false unity that the possibility of reacquiring primeval unity opens up.

In what way, however, are the diverse heterological moments, the figures of exteriority, an image of the origin? The critico-dialectic exegesis of Benjamin's thought—Adorno's first of all—has always vigorously insisted on the impossibility of articulating in a meaningful way the traits of this exteriority, which is to say to give a name to the utopia of the other. Now, this critical problem, even as it justifies itself against the risk that the totalizing mediation of the field of immanence might swallow whole whatever would wish to transcend it, is obligated to take account of the evidence that often, irresistibly, exteriority and the totally Other have, in Benjamin, the same connotations as the origin. There is in Benjamin something analogous to the Levinasian tension between totality and infinity, or perhaps to the tension Rosenzweig posits between the world of creation and the world of redemption. As in Emmanuel Levinas and Franz Rosenzweig, these extremes are not in dialectical tension. In other words, the Infinite and redemption are not evoked, in a Hegelian manner, by the contradictions of the totality. Rather, there is a radical asymmetry between the two poles which, rigorously speaking, are not even in relation one with the other. The pole of alterity, that which ruptures the connection of immanence, is always in Benjamin a figure of the origin, something that leads to a virtuality, a latency in being, that

1 We might consider Adorno's 'negative dialectic' as the attempt to speculatively translate into the language of the concept the irreducible exteriority of the Other in Benjamin's thought.

precedes the constitution of fallen reality, that of humanity after being driven from Eden. The messianic figure of the Other has, in Benjamin, the contours, above all, of that which interrupts the network of pragmatic, quotidian significations, the Bergsonian domination of matter, of utilitarian and self-conserving relations among human beings. We can inventory some moments of this Other's appearance. As we recalled at the start, what is at stake is the Goethean ideal of the archetypes which, in their discontinuity, their discrete and eternal character, burst in to counterbalance the exhausting, narcissistic reflexivity of romantic form, which is always about to degenerate into arbitrarily abstract and subjective significations.[2] Again, it will be a matter of the force of the *Ausdruckslose* (expressionless): the retardant element, the caesura, the idea of prose, which break the false appearance of the beautiful (understood, as in Gundolf, as an absolute, pacified reality). This happens on the basis of a dictate characteristic of all Benjamin's aesthetics, from the youthful essay on Hölderlin, through the work on the *Elective Affinities*, to the critique of the auratic artwork which, rather than coming from a materialistic conception, may be interpreted on the basis of the *Ausdruckslose*, of totality shattered. In addition, on a more specifically metaphysical plain, there will be the opposition, in the epistemological premise to *The Origin of German Tragic Drama*, between the sphere of ideas and the sphere of concepts.

Here too, the world of ideas, as a metaphysical refiguration of the Goethean world of 'originary phenomena', is characterized by its infinite transcendence of the conventional sphere of conceptual mediation. Decisive and exemplary is the rupture that takes place with a certain hierarchical and scholastic tradition of Platonism, which perceived in ideas a sort of all-encompassing concept. In Benjamin instead, there is an intensive and genetic vision of the idea: the intelligible is not the super-ordinate, that which disposes and regulates the universe of concepts. In other words, it is never thought of in terms of *archē*, as an

2 There is here something like a vindication of the atemporality of the classic in the face of the bad, progressive temporality of the romantic.

active principle of organization of knowledge. There is an inexhaustible richness of the idea as *Ursprung* that prohibits it from being misunderstood as generality, a statistical median of the specificity of phenomena. There is a Levinasian 'illeity', an alterity of the idea that impedes any reversibility, any bi-univocality of the relations between the empirical and the intelligible. As anarchic *Ursprung*, this alterity would flee from any proportionality, any synchrony of the relation between phenomena and the idea. Thus the refusal to conceive it as an intuitive vision, a mimetic relation that would be hierarchical and oppositional. There is no creative poeticity in the idea with respect to phenomena. Here resides all the difference between Benjamin and Goethean mythical naturalism, which, still following the long line of scholastic-Aristotelian descendancy, postulates instead a creative dimension in the world of archetypes. In Benjamin, the *Ursprung* is not a matrix that generates phenomena; rather, it is the place of their redemption, the horizon in which they become illuminated and acquire meaning. The *Ursprung* is not a projection into the future, but rather a recompense of the present in an immemorable past. From this point of view, the epistemological prologue thoroughly illuminates the meaning of all the alterities which, in Benjamin's thought, arise to break the immanent connections of the world of guilt—an abstract domain of conventional significations which comes after the separation between language and world.

The asymmetry, the shifting of the idea as origin with respect to the world of phenomena, configures a link between the intelligible world and the sensible world which is not mimetic, exemplary, and poetic (archetypal) but rather one we might call méthetic,[3] participatory and passive. Benjamin's utopia is not simply the empty hollow of the critique of totality. Utopia is the end of the constructive and generative ideal of knowledge. This implies the end of any subjection of phenomena to categorial predication, the suspension of the judging word. Knowledge no longer organizes phenomena, which, once liberated, are readmitted to

3 From *methexis*, the relationship of participation between a particular and a form in Plato's philosophy. [Trans.]

the truth of the origin. Paradoxically, the idea no longer belongs to the field of vision, the *theorein*, with subjective consciousness striving to grasp the world. Rather, idea here signifies listening, the flowing of phenomena back towards the call of their sensory root. In Benjamin, the idea as *Ursprung* is not a pure and simple reprise of Platonism mediated by scholastic thought, and neither is it a paganizing, generative source of phenomenicity, as shown by the polemic with the Warburg School and the accusation of mythicity levied at Goethe's thought. The *Ursprung* is, rather, a vortex that irresistibly pulls back into memory the phenomena left in their most complete passivity, no longer organized constructively to conceal their sensible matrix. The intelligible that breaks the network of false mediations constituting totality is thus revealed finally as nakedness, pure being exposed to the sensible. In contrast to the entire idealistic tradition, the absolute here is not at all a result, a product of human spiritual activity, understood as a fully unfolded autonomy of human consciousness. The absolute which is to be remembered, the absolute that speaks in the awareness of alterity, is rather ineffectual and limited in extent: root, virtuality, latency. In this way Benjamin succeeded in developing a personal and extremely original reading of the Neo-Kantian tradition and, most of all, of Hermann Cohen's philosophy of the origin. The perspectival vanishing point of Kantian metaphysics with respect to the universe of phenomenal representation is not only, and no longer, that which reaches out towards ultra-sensible ideas. Rather, the movement that interests Benjamin is towards a thing-in-itself that comes before the phenomenal-representational articulation of the sensible universe. The intelligible universe and the thing-in-itself are not the distillate, the quintessence, of representation: rather, for Benjamin, thing-in-itself would literally be the fall, the collapse, of the forms that organize the appropriation of the world through the operation of consciousness.

Benjamin's youthful neo-Kantianism will thus increasingly relinquish any blandly spiritual temptation, any positivist philosophy of values, to articulate itself finally against the categorical tendency of a priori forms, like a paradoxical neo-Kantian 'philosophy of the informal', a discovery of the intelligible in the very heart of sensibility. Evil and error are not inherent in the natural root of humankind, but in the organization and construction to which mankind subjects this root. Benjamin's path towards this sensible 'informal' here approaches, from several perspectives, the Machian and, more generally, the empirico-critical ideal of the *perceptio clara et confusa*, that is, the Husserlian ideal of pre-categorical evidence.[4] There is the by no means negligible difference, however, that Benjamin's *Ursprung*, by the force of its eminently linguistic character, carries the sign of an ineliminable historicity. Note that this historicity is not extrinsic to truth, to the 'illeity' of the idea, but is the very mode of its diachronic offering, its exterior being. The utopia of the informal has an intrinsic historical character. At the end of his early epistemological-linguistic reflections, in order to open up space for a requalification of the then-neglected notion of allegory and indicate the utopian potential of the informal, Benjamin abandons the still neo-Kantian notion of symbol to undertake, under the sign of history, this passage from a spiritualistic idea of transcendence—which can still be mediated and recuperated at the level of totality—to the recognition of the absolute alterity of transcendence and the discovery of its root in the sensible. The world of the Kingdom's absolute alterity with respect to the profane order flees from the somehow always representative index of the symbol—which etymologically 'holds together' what is actually radical disjunction and can only be indicated by the 'saying other' of allegory. In the passage from symbol to allegory, Benjamin achieves his comprehensive detachment from any critical idealism which would reduce alterity to the measure of any given intentional knowledge. This is precisely what 'symbolic' knowledge is, and as in general with Neo-Kantianism, it can never free itself from the prison of phenomenal representation.

At the transcendent pole of exteriority, what Benjamin wants is not to display the possibility of the Other and thus allude to it, but rather to experience its already somehow existent reality. If we wish to speak of

4 See the analysis by Manfred Sommer, *Lebenswelt und Zeitbewusstein* (Frankurt am Main: Suhrkamp, 1990).

Benjamin's 'materialism' in this regard, it would not consist in a more or less complete agreement with certain Marxian theories, but in this change in the direction of sensiblility, in the philosophical anthropology underpinning what we have called 'thinking the informal'. This change in direction is evoked in the opposition, upon which the prologue to *The Origin of German Tragic Drama* insists, between knowledge and truth. The order of truth is ultimately extra-representative, withdrawing from the dominion—both despotic and illusory—of consciousness which suffocatingly imposes its forms on things. Truth, as transcendence that breaks in to shatter the dominion of judging consciousness—of the knowledge of good and evil that has elevated itself over the world of things—is for Benjamin first of all an 'undoing the forms'. His book on the *Origin*, in which converge and resolve themselves the different drives of Benjamin's early thought, is above all something like a philosophy of *Enstaltung* (deformation). We should not be deceived here by the fact that the baroque world—the object of the book's inquiry—is plainly the terrain of metamorphosis *per excellence*, of the incessant mutation of forms. For Benjamin in fact, this metamorphosis, this changing of forms, is in turn precisely and solely allegory. Allegory of something that is still more profound and radical: allegory of a passage to a state that is, nirvana-like, *para-rūpa*[5]—beyond, or perhaps it would be better to say, on this side, of any form. At numerous points in his theoretical work, Benjamin has left traces that permit us to access this world of the 'without form'. The most fertile formulation of all this is, however, certainly what we find in the overall project of the *Berlin Childhood* and, in theoretical terms, in the 'Thought Figures' (especially the 'Short Shadows' of the Ibiza period). This is what, in a broad sense and paraphrasing Benjamin's 'metaphysics of youth', we might call his 'metaphysics of infancy'.

5 Writing on the origin and use of the images of angels in Hinduism, Cooramaswamy notes that 'the image per se is neither God nor any angel, but merely an aspect or hypostasis (*avasthā*) of God, who is in the last analysis without likeness (*amūrta*), not determined by form (*arūpa*), trans-form (*para-rūpa*).' Ananda K. Coomaraswamy, *The Transformation of Nature in Art* (New York: Dover, 1956[1934]), p. 157. [Trans.]

The most well-known motif of this metaphysics of infancy is certainly Benjamin's theory of the name, the critique of the abstract signifying word that reigns in post-Edenic human commerce. This critique aims at dismantling form as the distinction, in the heart of language, between signifier and signified, signification and object, in order to recuperate the infancy, etymologically speaking, of humanity before the Fall, when language is neither convention nor onomatopoeia, because it does not refer to something outside itself. The philosophy of the informal follows the path that Benjamin defined as the '*streben ins Innere*' (striving inwards),[6] the plunging of the subject into the purest, most radical possible primeval passivity. Among the most important places for this re-ascension, beyond representational appearances, into radical diachrony—the anarchy of being on this side of form—there is undoubtedly the Benjaminian theory of colours, which is found not only in many parts of his writing about infancy (including *Berlin Childhood*) but also in the aesthetic notations towards a theory of *Phantasie* contained in the 'Fragment' of the sixth volume of his collected works.[7]. The theory of colour is in every way the equivalent of the linguistic theory of the name, within the realm of a single anthropology of originary sensibility. It is here that the theory of the *Enstaltung*, thanks to the extreme opposition between form and colour, finds not only its most complete development, but also its most persuasive. It is a crucial theoretical moment because it fully reveals the distance of Benjamin's thought from any metaphysics of intuition, any neo-pagan naturalism; the impossibility of it being confused with Goethean Platonism or with the irrationalism of the 'Kosmiker'[8] (despite the indubitable affinities with Klages). It is here that we can fully understand the notifications in the prologue to *The Origin of German Tragic Drama* that the idea as *Ursprung* can never manifest in an intuitive vision of images, *bildhafte*.[9]

---

6 Benjamin, 'Zur Ästhetik' in *Gesammelte Schriften*, VOL. 6, p. 109.

7 Benjamin, 'Zur Ästhetik' in *Gesammelte Schriften*, VOL. 6, pp. 109–25. The expression *Entstaltung des Gestalten* (deformation of forms) is found on p. 114.

8 A reference to the Munich Cosmic Circle, Kosmikerkreis, a group of writers and intellectuals that included the philosopher Ludwig Klages. [Trans.]

9 See Chapter 3, Section 2 above. [Trans.]

Benjamin's *Phantasie* is, per excellence, imagination without images, matrix, source, grasped in its pure potentiality, on this side of its self-objectification. The *Phantasie* that reveals itself in its purity, in an absolutely unintentional contemplation of colour, such as that experienced by children before they are made subject to forms and meanings, is therefore the exact opposite of a free, unfurled creativity. '*Unschöpferisch*' (uncreative) is how Benjamin precisely defines it.[10] It is '*reine Empfängnis*' (pure conception), born from the 'genius of oblivion'.[11] Its force is not that of production but of ascesis. 'Without images', as one of the memorable 'Short Shadows' puts it, it is 'the refuge of all images'.[12] Benjamin's utopia of the Other is not, therefore, negative in the sense in which this absence of images has often been misunderstood by critical theory. It is not at all devoid of contents and its utopian potential is not given only in critique, by the tension between the existent and that which the existent should be. Perhaps there has been a fear of taking what he is saying literally, because no utopia has ever been constructed out of such a paradoxical positivity. No longer as allegory, in fact, but in pure literality is how we should take a utopia whose form is that of not having any, whose image is to be the very place of the absence of images.

---

10 Benjamin, 'Zur Ästhetik' in *Gesammelte Schriften*, VOL. 6, p. 109.

11 Benjamin, 'Zur Ästhetik' in *Gesammelte Schriften*, VOL. 6, pp. 116–17.

12 Benjamin, 'Short Shadows (I)' in *SW*, VOL. 2, PART 1, p. 269.

Chronology of the Life and Works of Walter Benjamin

1892 Birth of Walter Benjamin in Berlin on 15 July to Jewish parents. His father, Emil, is an art and antiquities dealer.

1902 W. B. begins attending the Friedrich-Wilhelm Gymnasium in Berlin's Charlottenburg neighbourhood. Among his schoolfellows are future friends Ernst Schoen, Alfred Cohn, Fritz Straus, and Herbert Blumenthal.

1905 For health reasons he interrupts his studies in Berlin, but continues at the Landerziehungsheim in Haubinda, Thuringia, until returning to Berlin in 1907. In Haubinda he experiences the educational methods of Gustav Wyneken, theorist of the 'new education'.

1912 Finishes secondary school. Writes under the pseudonym 'Ardour' for the periodical 'Der Anfang', a vehicle for the followers of Wyneken directed by Georg Gretor and Sigfried Bernfeld. Enrols at the University of Berlin, but for the summer session transfers to the University of Freiburg i.B., where he becomes friends with poet C. F. Heinle.

1913 Visits Paris for the first time, returning to Berlin in September.

1914 Serves as president of the Berlin 'Free Student' association, characterized by its critical attitude towards German nationalism. Exonerated from military service due to a nervous condition. Meets Dora Sophie Kellner, his future wife.

1915 While collaborating on 'Der Anfang', he completes over the winter the study 'Two Poems by Hölderlin' and continues to study philosophy in Munich. Meets Gershom Scholem, the future great scholar of Jewish mysticism.

1916 Beginning of his relationship with Dora Sophie Pollak, who is separated from her husband. Follows courses by Americanist Walter Lehmann and phenomenologist Moritz Geiger. Meets Rilke in passing. Writes the essay 'On Language as Such and On the Language of Man'.

1917 Marries Dora Pollak. The couple moves to Switzerland. Benjamin decides to obtain a degree at the University of Bern with prof. Richard Herbertz.

1918 His son Stefan Rafael is born.

1919 Obtains the title of Doctor in Philosophy, discussing his thesis on 'The Concept of Criticism in German Romanticism', which will be published the following year. Through the mediation of Hugo Ball, he meets Ernst Bloch.

1920 Returns to Berlin, moving back in to the paternal household.

1921 His marriage is in crisis, as Dora has fallen in love with Ernst Schoen and Benjamin with Jula Cohn. Publishes the essay 'Toward the Critique of Violence'. Buys Paul Klee's watercolour *Angelus Novus*. He proposes creating a journal with the same title to be published by Weissbach, but it never sees the light. He becomes close to F. C. Rang.

1923 Publishes the translation of Baudelaire's *Tableaux parisiens* with Weissbach, with the important essay 'The Task of the Translator' as preface. Meets Theodor W. Adorno through the mediation of Kracauer.

1924 From May to October he lives in Capri in the company of Ernst Bloch and Erich and Lucie Gutkind. In the summer he meets Asja Lacis, a Russian revolutionary from Riga, under whose influence he will encounter Marxism. In the meantime he works on his book on German baroque drama. The first part of the essay on 'Goethe's *Elective Affinities*' comes out in Hugo von Hoffmannstahl's literary magazine *Neue Deutsche Beiträge*.

1925 His effort to obtain a faculty position at the University of Frankfurt on the strength of his work on *The Origin of German Tragic Drama* comes to naught. From this point on Benjamin will make his living as a free-lance essayist, translator, and writer for newspapers and journals such as the *Frankfurter Zeitung* and *Die literarische Welt*. With Franz Hessel he plans a project for a German edition of Marcel Proust's *In Search of Lost Time*. The second part of his essay on 'Goethe's *Elective Affinities*' is published.

1926 Benjamin's father dies. He moves to Paris to work on the Proust translation. In early December he moves to Moscow where Asja Lacis awaits him.

1927 Returns to Berlin from Moscow at the beginning of February. A diary kept during his Russian experience will be published posthumously. Reading Aragon's *Le paysan de Paris* provides the decisive impulse for the project of a work on the Parisian 'Passages'. With various friends he begins to experiment with drugs and hashish.

1928 Publishes *The Origin of German Tragic Drama* and *One-Way Street*, a collection of aphorisms, with Rowohlt.

1929 Meets Bertolt Brecht; the two become fast friends. Publishes his important essay 'Surrealism'.

1930 Obtains a divorce from Dora.

1931 Publishes the essay 'The Destructive Character'.

1932 Moves to Ibiza. Writes the series of aphorisms entitled 'Short Shadows'.

1933 In March he moves into voluntary exile in Paris. Another sojourn in Ibiza. Begins publishing in Germany under the pseudonym Detlef Holz. Publishes the essay 'Experience and Poverty'.

1934 From July to October he is a guest of Bertolt Brecht in Denmark, in Skovbostrand, near Svendborg. In the *Zeitschrift für*

Sozialforschung, organ of the Institute for Social Research in its new base in Paris, he publishes the essay 'The Present Social Situation of the French Writer'. Publishes his essay on Kafka in the *Jüdische Rundschau*. In October he moves to Sanremo, living in a pension run by Dora, his divorced wife.

1935 Returns to Paris in February where he becomes a funded member of the Institute for Social Research.

1936 Second visit to Denmark, staying with Brecht. Vain efforts to obtain French citizenship. His essay on 'The Work of Art in the Age of Its Technological Reproducibility' comes out in a French translation by P. Klossowski in *Zeitchrift für Sozialforschung*. The Lucerne publisher Vita Nova releases Benjamin's *Deutsche Menschen*, the collection of letters from the period between 1783 and 1883, under the pseudonym Detlef Holz. Publication of the important essay 'The Storyteller'.

1937 The essay on 'Eduard Fuchs, Collector and Historian' appears in the Institute's journal.

1938 Once again in Denmark with Brecht. He meets with Adorno for the final time in Sanremo.

1939 From September to November he is interned as a German citizen in the concentration camp in Nevers. The essay 'On Some Motifs in Baudelaire' comes out in the *Zeitschrift für Sozialforschung*.

1940 Writes the theses 'On the Concept of History'. Obtains a visa to move to the United States. Facing the Nazi advance, Benjamin leaves Paris in June. In September he attempts to cross the Pyrenees into Spain. Stopped by the police, who threaten to hand him over to the Germans. During the night between 26 and 27 September, Benjamin commits suicide by ingesting a massive dose of morphine. The little group of fugitives who had been travelling with him receive their visas to pass into Spain.

History of Criticism

It certainly cannot be claimed that Walter Benjamin's theoretical work developed in isolation, without exchange and communication with his contemporaries. If anything, the opposite is the case, as Adorno was first to recognize.[1] There is no twentieth century philosophical or literary current that Benjamin did not take the measure of. In a characteristic manner, this is especially true with regard to positions that are in some way antagonistically opposed to one another, sometimes diametrically. Thus Benjamin was able to dialogue simultaneously with the aestheticism of Stefan George and Hugo von Hoffmannstahl no less than with Brecht's politically militant poetry. He had as interlocutors the leading theoreticians of western Marxism—Lukács and Bloch—no less than exponents of right-wing political decisionism such as Carl Schmitt. He attempted to enter into contact with exponents of the Warburg School no less that with the most eminent figures of new twentieth century Jewish thought, from Scholem to Rosenzweig, not to mention his more noted and difficult relation with the Institute for Social Research during the period of his emigration. In the face of such open communication and dialogical engagement, as revealed especially in his letters, we cannot fail to be surprised at the scantiness of critical discussion on Benjamin while the author was alive. This is due to various motives. *The Origin of German Tragic Drama*, the only complete work accomplished by Benjamin except for his short collection of aphorisms, 'One-Way Street', went practically unreviewed, in part because of its philosophical inaccessibility to the world of literary criticism, and in part because its topic found little interest among philosophers. The rest of Benjamin's production appeared

1 Theodor W. Adorno, *Über Walter Benjamin* (Frankfurt am Main: Suhrkamp, 1990[1970]), pp. 68–69.

in scattered and fragmentary form in journals and periodicals, rendering virtually impossible a complete or comprehensive reading of his thought. Lastly, there are the factors of the travail of exile and his tragic death at the beginning of the Second World War.

Among the few exceptions, we should take note, for its depth, of the joint review of the *Origin* and 'One-Way Street' that appeared in the 15 July 1928 *Frankfurter Zeitung* by Sigfried Kracauer.[2] In only a few pages, Kracauer anticipates several fundamental elements of future Benjamin reception. Kracauer insists especially on the unity of Benjamin's thought, manifest across works that appear radically heterogeneous to one another.

> Despite their thematic differences, the two works belong together as expressions of a type of thinking that is foreign to current thought. Such thinking is more akin to Talmudic writings and medieval tractates, for, like these, its manner of presentation [*Darstellungsform*] is interpretation. Its intentions are of a theological sort.[3]

Moving along this horizon, Kracauer seeks to bring into relief the double movement in Benjamin's thought: the movement of critique, the breaking down of false categorical unities, and the one dedicated to the saving of phenomena.

> Whereas abstraction links phenomena with one another in order to arrange them in a more or less systematic context of formal concepts, Benjamin avails himself of Scholasticism and the Platonic doctrine of ideas in order to assert the discontinuous multiplicity, not so much of phenomena, but of ideas. These manifest themselves in the murky medium of history. The tragic drama, for instance, is an idea.[4]

---

2 See Siegfried Kracauer, 'On the Writings of Water Benjamin' in *The Mass Ornament: Weimar Essays* (Thomas Y. Levin trans. and ed.) (Cambridge, MA: Harvard University Press, 1995), pp. 259–66.

3 Kracauer, 'On the Writings of Water Benjamin', p. 259.

4 Kracauer, 'On the Writings of Water Benjamin', p. 259.

In his reading, Kracauer emphasizes how such an approach necessitates burning any bridges that falsely promise immediacy; thus the indispensability of criticism in order to reveal the idea. 'He who faces the world in its immediacy is presented with a figure to be smashed in order to reach the essentialities.'[5] Kracauer highlights the importance of Benjamin's rediscovery of allegory as an exemplary incarnation of an operation aimed at the dissolution of false categorial unities, so as to bring the essence into light. 'Where meanings come together under the sign of an idea, rather than being "sublated" into a formal concept, they come together like sparks of electricity.'[6] This work of selection, which pertains appropriately to a criticism that contemplates the atemporal order of the world of ideas, is for Kracauer of an exquisitely theological nature.

> For Benjamin, the world is obscured and obstructed, in the way that it always has been from a theological perspective. This is also precisely the basis for Benjamin's belief that it is not necessary to respect the immediate—that the façade must be torn down, and form cut to pieces.[7]

This work of destruction[8] is the initial premise to bring into focus the second aspect of Benjamin's theoretical work: the mission to redeem phenomena, which are finally led back into the gravitational orbit of the ideal order of ideas. 'Empowered by his insights into this order, Benjamin wishes to carry out an act of redemption appropriate to theological contemplation. His particular concern is always to demonstrate that big matters are small and small matters big.'[9] Kracauer describes how Benjamin's criticism discovers—contrary to conventional mediation, according which everything amalgamates and blends together—the latent and almost invisible forces of 'redemption'. 'The divining rod of

---

5 Kracauer, 'On the Writings of Water Benjamin', p. 260.

6 Kracauer, 'On the Writings of Water Benjamin', p. 260.

7 Kracauer, 'On the Writings of Water Benjamin', p. 261.

8 See Walter Benjamin, 'The Destructive Character' in *SW*, VOL. 2, PART 2, pp. 541–42. See also Gerard Raulet, *Le caractère destructeur* (Paris: Flammarion, 1997).

9 Kracauer, 'On the Writings of Water Benjamin', p. 262.

his intuition strikes upon the realm of the inconspicuous, the realm of the generally deprecated, the realm that history has passed over, and it is precisely here that it discovers the greatest significance.'[10] The contemplation of the order of the essences thus becomes 'the uncovering of those hidden moments and nodal points in the course of history where salvation is intended or appears in the image.'[11] A final motif, which will later become dominant in 'On the Concept of History', is anticipated in Kracauer's precocious recognition of the idea of the redemption of the past. 'His proper material is what has been: for Benjamin, knowledge arises out of ruins. Thus, there is no attempt here to redeem the living world; instead, the meditator redeems fragments of the past.'[12]

Starting from the 1930s, the condition of exile and the fragmentary state of his work reduce the fortunes of Benjamin's thought almost to a clandestine status, limited to very few, privileged intellectual interlocutors, who also happen to be quite diverse among themselves.[13] This is true to such an extent that in the mid-1960s Gershom Scholem, Benjamin's oldest friend, could legitimately write about the reception of Benjamin that,

> A life which unfolded entirely outside the public stage, although linked to it through his activity as writer, fell into complete oblivion except for those very few who had had an unforgettable impression of him. In the more than twenty years passed between the advent of the Nazi era in Germany and the publication, in 1955, of a collection including most of his key writings, his name has been one of the most forgotten in the spiritual world.[14]

---

10 Kracauer, 'On the Writings of Water Benjamin', p. 262.

11 Kracauer, 'On the Writings of Water Benjamin', p. 262.

12 Kracauer, 'On the Writings of Water Benjamin', p. 264.

13 In the experience of exile in Paris, of particular importance are his contacts with critics who come out of surrealism (Pierre Klossowski and Georges Bataille) and with the circle around André Gide (especially the critic Charles Du Bos).

14 Scholem's testimony is found in *Über Walter Benjamin* (1968), p. 132.

Today, notwithstanding the polemics beginning in the sixties coming from orthodox Marxists against the 2-volume edition overseen by Adorno,[15] there is no doubt that without this initiative, Benjamin's writings would have run the risk of being scattered entirely. This remains true independently of Adorno's editorial intention to shift Benjamin's late thought into the background, as he considered it bound to Marxist orthodoxy and determined by the influence of Bertolt Brecht. Since the era of his habilitation work on Kierkegaard (1933), Adorno had made use of innumerable of Benjamin's categories—from the concept of 'natural history' to that of *Schuldzusammenhang* (context of guilt), from that of 'constellation' to that of 'aura', just for a couple of examples—but he also contributed decisively to the postwar rediscovery of Benjamin's thought. Adorno's contributions, with standouts such as his 1950 essay later collected in *Prisms* and the *Introduction* to the 1955 edition of the *Schriften*,[16] are characterized by the tact and discretion with which he approaches the figure of Benjamin, evoking motifs and figures of his thought across a spectrum without presuming to tie together the threads of a philosophy which, after youthful hesitation, had decisively proceeded upon an unsystematic path. Adorno's essays on Benjamin are so many moments in a single exercise we may call physiognomic. Throughout, acknowledging the turbid and confused mixture that had already been pointed out by Kracauer, Adorno insists above all on the incommensurability of Benjamin's thought with regard to the categories and concepts of professional philosophy. 'Benjamin's thoughts shimmer with a light that

---

15 For a review of these criticisms, see Klaus Garber, 'Étapes de la reception de Benjamin' in Heinz Wismann (ed.), *Walter Benjamin et Paris* (Paris: Cerf, 1986), pp. 941ff.

16 Theodor W. Adorno, 'Charakteristik Walter Benjamin' first appeared on the tenth anniversary of his death in *Die Neue Rundschau* 61(4) 1950: 571–84; English translation: 'A Portrait of Walter Benjamin' in *Prisms* (Samuel and Shierry Weber trans.) (Cambridge, MA: MIT Press, 1981), pp. 227–41; Theodor W. Adorno, 'Einleitung zu Benjamins Schriften' in *Walter Benjamin*: *Schriften* (Theodor W. Adorno and Gretel Adorno eds) (Frankfurt am Main: Suhrkamp, 1955), VOL. 1, pp. *vii–xxvii*; English translation: 'Introduction to Benjamin's *Schriften*' in Smith (ed.), *On Walter Benjamin*, pp. 2–17.

does not appear in the spectrum of concepts, a light that belongs to an order which the conscience immediately wishes to ward off so as not to feel the disgust of the familiar world and its purposes.'[17] To define this characteristic admixture and the rupturing of mediality, Adorno makes constant recourse to oxymorons that express the co-presence of extremes in Benjamin's thought, specifically the extremity of phenomena to be redeemed and the extremity of the realm of ideas in which their redemption may be realized. This co-presence of extremes, however, already marks Benjamin's thought on a stylistic level. 'What Benjamin said and wrote sounded as though it were coming from secrecy. But it took all its force from evidence.'[18] This stylistic characteristic leads us back to the essential quality of Benjamin's philosophy: 'As little as it allows sensuous happiness, prohibited by the traditional morals of work, Benjamin's thought also denies itself its spiritual antithesis, the relation with the absolute. In fact, the beyond-nature is inseparable from the fulfilment of what is natural.'[19] It is precisely due to this co-presence, Adorno claims, that transcendence is grasped by Benjamin in an oblique and discontinuous manner, which is to say allegorically. 'He strives towards the absolute, but in a broken line, through mediation.'[20] Pursuing this viewpoint, Adorno can characterize Benjamin's as a thought that does not develop randomly, obedient to an impulse towards abstract philosophizing. On the contrary, Benjamin's thought is concrete, nourished on experience and the mediation of texts. Benjamin's work takes place under the sign of a secularization of theology which reads profane texts as though they were sacred. What flows from this is a consideration of Benjamin's philosophy as essentially hermeneutic. 'All creation transforms for him into writing, which attempts to decipher a code that is unknown. He plunges into reality as though into a palimpsest. Interpretation, translation, critique are the schemata of his thought.'[21] Among the themes

17 Adorno, *Über Walter Benjamin*, p. 35.

18 Adorno, *Über Walter Benjamin*, p. 35.

19 Adorno, *Über Walter Benjamin*, p. 35.

20 Adorno, *Über Walter Benjamin*, p. 38.

21 Adorno, *Über Walter Benjamin*, p. 41.

pertaining to Benjamin's philosophy, Adorno has pointed out above all that of 'natural history', which is as central to the book on German tragic drama as it is to Benjamin's subsequent reflections on the character of late-capitalist society. For Adorno, this is the context in which to situate the drive in Benjamin's thought to become image:

> The character of image in Benjamin's speculation, his mythicizing trait, if you like, derives precisely from the way that, under his meditative gaze, the historical element is transformed into nature by force of its own caducity, while every natural element is transformed into a moment of the history of creation.[22]

In greater detail, Adorno differentiates Benjamin's idea of image from Jung and Klages' conception of archetypal images, insisting on the dialectic dimension of Benjamin's image, which is to say its historical rootedness. This is after all, according to Adorno, the meaning of Benjamin's 'dialectic in a state of quietude'. Thanks to this idea, 'Benjamin escaped from the antithesis between the eternal and the historical through a micro-logical procedure, by concentrating on what is most minuscule, where historical movement is suspended and becomes sedimented in image.'[23]

All this confers an 'athematic' character on Benjamin's thought overall. 'Dialectic at a standstill defines his philosophy in the degree to which it recognizes in itself no time of development, but receives its form as a constellation of individual enunciations.'[24] In this sense, then, Adorno celebrated Benjamin's thought as a force capable of escaping any social convention and, in its incessant generosity, able to throw open the wonder of the new, discovering unknown worlds. 'He had a particular faculty which, in its ability to bring happiness, retained within itself, in an infinitely profound manner, any purely immediate force: the faculty to give without limits.'[25] Adorno's most original theoretical contributions

22 Adorno, *Über Walter Benjamin*, pp. 41–42.

23 Adorno, *Über Walter Benjamin*, p. 44.

24 Adorno, *Über Walter Benjamin*, p. 46.

25 Adorno, *Über Walter Benjamin*, p. 49.

in discussing Benjamin's work are probably those found in the correspondence of the years of emigration, all relating to Benjamin's work as collaborator at the Institute for Social Research.[26]

Of particular interest in this context, beyond Adorno's description of the supposed limits of Benjamin's materialism (Adorno had accused his friend of sociologism and determinism in the 10 November 1938 letter discussing the first draft of the essay on Baudelaire),[27] is the aesthetic discussion around Benjamin's essay 'The Work of Art in the Age of Its Technological Reproducibility', contained in Adorno's letter of 18 March 1936.[28] In this letter Adorno attempts to speculatively re-dialecticize the extremes which, he feels, Benjamin's magical sociologism has wrongly fixed in place: on one side the concept of 'aura', of the cultic or traditional work of art; on the other the concept of the disenchanted artwork, its aura removed and technologically reproducible. As Adorno sees it, the logic of disenchantment that underlies Benjamin's discourse is victim to the 'dialectic of clarification'. The aura, in fact the veil that circumscribes the autonomy of the traditional artwork, does not constitute a cultic residue at all. On the contrary, for Adorno the aura is the objectification of a distance from the cultic; it is the element thanks to which art distinguishes itself from magic, with which it has in common its genesis in the mimetic element.[29] The aura is not an element of myth in the artwork, the distancing from a primeval rituality. Contrary to what Benjamin claims, the aura is for Adorno the dimension which, better than any other, defines the irreducibility of the aesthetic space, which stands apart from myth but also conserves the echo of it.

---

26 In particular, the letters dated 17 December 1934, 2 August 1935, 18 March 1936, 10 November 1938, 1 February 1939 and 29 February 1940. See Theodor W. Adorno and Walter Benjamin, *The Complete Correspondence, 1928–1940* (Henri Lonitz ed., Nicholas Walker trans.) (Cambridge, MA: Harvard University Press, 1999).

27 Adorno and Benjamin, *Complete Correspondence*, pp. 280–89.

28 Adorno and Benjamin, *Complete Correspondence*, pp. 127–34.

29 Adorno and Benjamin, *Complete Correspondence*, pp. 129.

In substance, the aura is that alone which provides for the salvation of the archaic, the mimetic residue eliminated from the bourgeois *ratio*, but it transforms that impulse into knowledge. The defence of the aura, which in Kantian terms would be the aesthetic appearance, has its speculative flipside in the attack on the other pole of Benjamin's discourse, the assumption (which Adorno charges with being fetishistically hypostasized in a technical sense) of the new aesthetic rationality inaugurated by the technologies of reproducibility. Adorno's critique here has a double aspect.[30] He wishes, on the one hand, to bring to light the aura, positive and cultic, of technicity left to itself, but on the other, more radically, he wants to denounce as pseudo-conciliation—behind which stands the reality of the process of social integration—the end of the aristocratic autonomy of art which is promised by those technological procedures. This false conciliation is called 'cultural industry'. Still, just as the defence of the aura does not mean the collapse into myth but rather its criticism, in the same way, the attack on the technological veil is not a refutation of the progress of aesthetic rationality. The process of 'spiritualization', of disenchantment, is an essential presupposition so that art may continue to insist on its own autonomy. Only by radicalizing the difference of its rationality from technical-scientific rationality can art posit, rather than the conditions of its social integration, the utopia of its realization.[31] In general, all the discussion that took place in the sixties following Adorno's publication of Benjamin's *Schriften* is characterized by the crushing predominance of a single theme, which was the significance of Benjamin's later work and his relation with Marxism. Leaving aside the polemical statements regarding the supposed censorship carried out by Adorno as editor of Benjamin's collected works,[32] among notable contributions we might mention in particular the reference to Benjamin in Lukács' 1963

30 Adorno and Benjamin, *Complete Correspondence*, pp. 130.

31 These are themes which, in constant dialogue with Benjamin, will be developed by Adorno in his *Aesthetic Theory*.

32 See in this regard, Klaus Garber, *Rezeption und Rettung* (Tübingen: Niemeyer, 1987), pp. 121–93.

The Specificity of the Aesthetic and Hannah Arendt's essay on Benjamin, published in 1968. Lukács discusses Benjamin's book on German baroque drama in the chapter in *The Specificity of the Aesthetic* entitled 'Allegory and Symbol', renewing his earlier criticisms while considering Benjamin the most lucid and coherent exponent of the avant-garde. Lukács criticizes Benjamin's aesthetics as being incapable of holding firmly to the principle of mirroring, focusing instead, through the exaltation of allegory, 'on the destruction of immediate, sensible reality.'[33] Although possessing a lucidity superior to that of his contemporaries and those with whom he had an affinity, Benjamin is deemed unable to avoid the nihilistic, anti-humanistic drift of the twentieth century avant-garde.

In a drastic form, with a polemical *vis* sharper than all the anti-Adornian bitterness of his Marxist critics, Hannah Arendt denounces the interpretation of Adorno and his school, especially in the figure of Rolf Tiedemann. Arendt rejects Benjamin's qualifications as a philosopher but acknowledges his stature as a philologist and poet. In this sense, the horizon of Benjamin's work is enclosed within a constellation represented by the apparently distant names of Goethe and Brecht.

> What fascinated him [. . .] was that the spirit and its material manifestation were so intimately connected that it seemed permissible to discover everywhere Baudelaire's *correspondances*, which clarified and illuminated one another if they were properly correlated, so that finally they would no longer require any interpretative or explanatory commentary.[34]

From this perspective, Arendt defends the first draft of the essay on Baudelaire, freeing it from the Adornian accusation of being merely a positivist enumeration of individual cases in point. In effect, it is precisely

---

33 György Lukács, *Estetica*, 2 VOLS (Turin: Einaudi, 1970), VOL. 2, p. 829. [This is an Italian translation of *Die Eigenart des Ästhetischen* (1963), only the first volume has been translated into English, as *The Specificity of the Aesthetic*, VOL. 1 (Erik M. Bachman and Tyrus Miller eds, Erik M. Bachman trans.) (Chicago: Haymarket, 2024). —Trans.]

34 Hannah Arendt, Introduction to Benjamin, *Illuminations*, p. 11.

the organization of the materials according to a method of correspondences that is itself dense with meaning. In this attention to the concrete, Arendt claims, Benjamin is truly close to Brecht, whose influence was judged as disastrous as much by Scholem as Adorno.

> In his concern with directly, actually demonstrable concrete facts, with single events and occurrences whose 'significance' is manifest, Benjamin was not much interested in theories or 'ideas' which did not immediately assume the most precise outward shape imaginable. To this very complex but still highly realistic mode of thought the Marxian relationship between superstructure and substructure became, in a precise sense, a metaphorical one.[35]

In response to Arendt's observations here, there remain only a few fragments of an unfinished text by Adorno, entitled 'Zur Interpretation Benjamins'.[36] Criticizing the patchwork and imprecise knowledge of Marx on the part both of Brecht and Benjamin, they nevertheless vindicate the integrally philosophical character of Benjamin's work.

> Principal thesis of H. A.: W. B. was not a philosopher. What kind of concept of philosophy! It is that of mister Heidegger, towards whom H. A. exercises that adulation which she wrongly attributes to Tiedemann towards me.—Show where the philosophy is. The concept of *critique* in W. B. is substantial only by force of its philosophical content; otherwise it would not have the emphatic force that raises B. above the familiar. By this model H. A. would like to rob him precisely of his paradigmatic quality.[37]

The reception of Benjamin's work on the part of Gershom Scholem took place completely outside the climate of such polemical bitterness, and

---

35 Arendt, Introduction to *Illuminations*, p. 13.

36 See Adorno, *Über Walter Benjamin*, pp. 97–100.

37 Adorno, *Über Walter Benjamin*, pp. 97–98.

his contribution to the rediscovery and re-evaluation of Benjamin is alone equal to that of Adorno. Scholem's treatment is found essentially in two volumes, *Walter Benjamin: The Story of a Friendship* (1975), and the collection *Walter Benjamin und sein Engel* (1983), which contains fourteen essays and smaller pieces. The direction of Scholem's investigations, which had the great merit of plumbing the most secret depths of Benjamin's work, is in any case already fully delineated in his first long essay on Benjamin, first published in 1965.[38] Agreeing with Adorno, Scholem sees Benjamin's work as pertaining to the realm of philosophy: 'Benjamin was a philosopher. He was a philosopher in all the phases of his work and in all the forms it assumes.'[39] To this general characterization, Scholem adds a specification of no secondary importance: 'Benjamin was a metaphysician. In fact I would add, the pure case of a metaphysician.'[40] What is however typical of Benjamin is the fact that this metaphysics is not laid out in its traditional setting, but rather starting from the experience of caducity and the ephemeral; from that which seems the very negation of metaphysics.

> Ever more energetically, he felt attracted to objects which seem to have little or nothing to do with metaphysics. What constitutes the particularity of his genius is the way in which, under his gaze, each of these objects reveals its own dignity and its own philosophical aura, to whose description he dedicated his efforts.[41]

This metaphysical gaze somehow signifies a sort of reversal with respect to the secularization of theology which Adorno had spoken of. 'In an unpredictable manner, the consideration of the profane realm passes over into the theological domain, even where it appears to be completely

38 Gershom Scholem, 'Walter Benjamin', *Die Neue Rundschau* 76(1) (1965): 1–21, later included in Adorno et. al, *Über Walter Benjamin*, pp. 132–64.

39 Scholem, 'Walter Benjamin' in Adorno et. al, *Über Walter Benjamin*, p. 138.

40 Scholem, 'Walter Benjamin' in Adorno et. al, *Über Walter Benjamin*, p. 138.

41 Scholem, 'Walter Benjamin' in Adorno et. al, *Über Walter Benjamin*, p. 139.

dissolved in the sphere of the mundane.'[42] Scholem recognizes this theological-metaphysical dimension even in the materialist turn taken by Benjamin in the 1930s, which Scholem for his part deprecates, just as Adorno did. 'Benjamin tried to position his dialectic, which was that of a theologian and metaphysician, on the same level as materialist dialectics, and he paid a very high price for this, I would say too high.'[43] Under the materialist coating, Scholem still sees a theological inspiration, and in particular Benjamin's closeness to the fundamental themes of the Judaic tradition, especially in terms of the philosophy of language and history. 'Two categories always surface anew at the centre of his writings, precisely in their Judaic versions: on the one hand, revelation, the idea of Torah, the representation of doctrine and the sacred texts in general; on the other, messianism and redemption.'[44] In Benjamin's materialist turn, the second of these two categories is conserved *expressis verbis*, but the first is also 'connected most tightly with its most characteristic procedure, the commentary on great and authoritative texts.'[45] Scholem's fundamental thesis can be summarized in the claim that Benjamin's thought 'had asymptotically come ever closer to Judaic thought, but without ever reaching it.'[46]

During the sixties, two of Peter Szondi's readings of Benjamin in an aesthetic-literary key played an important role in the reception of his work. The first appeared in the 8 October 1961 *Neue Zürcher Zeitung* under the title 'Hoffnung im Vergangenen' ('Hope in the Past'), while the second, dated 1961–1962, appeared as an afterword to Benjamin's *Städtebilder*.[47] The first essay distinguishes Benjamin's position with respect

42 Scholem, 'Walter Benjamin' in Adorno et. al, *Über Walter Benjamin*, p. 144.

43 Scholem, 'Walter Benjamin' in Adorno et. al, *Über Walter Benjamin*, p. 157.

44 Scholem, 'Walter Benjamin' in Adorno et. al, *Über Walter Benjamin*, p. 157.

45 Scholem, 'Walter Benjamin' in Adorno et. al, *Über Walter Benjamin*, p. 158.

46 Scholem, 'Walter Benjamin' in Adorno et. al, *Über Walter Benjamin*, p. 162.

47 See Péter Szondi, 'Hope in the Past: On Walter Benjamin' (Harvey Mendelsohn trans.), *Critical Inquiry* 4(3) (1978): 491–506; and 'Walter Benjamin's City Portraits (1962)' (Harvey Mendelsohn trans.) in Smith (ed.), *On Walter Benjamin*, pp. 18–32.

to Proust: Szondi recognizes in Benjamin's conception of the past, as realized in *Berlin Childhood around 1900*, not so much an effort to abolish time through remembrance, as in Proust, but rather an attempt to individuate within the past the signs and traces that might reveal the future. 'Benjamin's tense is not the perfect, but the future perfect in the fullness of its paradox: being future and past at the same.'[48] Szondi sees Benjamin's work as centred on his ability to find correspondences, images, and metaphors capable of safeguarding their prophetic power in the past.

> In Benjamin as well simile can assist memory when it seeks tokens of the future in the past. In such instances, the two members of the simile are related as a text that one actually experiences is related to its prophetic commentary, which is first deciphered by memory.[49]

What stands for the relation between past and future stands equally for the experience of estrangement, the experience of traveling.

> It is metaphor that makes Benjamin's city portraits what they are. It is the source of their magic and, in a very precise sense, their status as poetic writing. The very purpose of these texts, to convey the experience of alienation and of being a foreigner, is first accomplished through the medium of language, which here is a language of images. The quest for lost time and for what takes its place is no less bound to language than the attempt to take possession of what one has already found. Name and image are the two poles of this field of force.[50]

Among the most interesting and acute interventions into the relation between Benjamin and Adorno, coming at the end of the sixties, is certainly the essay 'Culture and Ideology' by Jacob Taubes.[51] Highlighting,

---

48 Szondi, 'Hope in the Past': 499.

49 Szondi, 'Walter Benjamin's City Portraits', p. 28.

50 Szondi, 'Walter Benjamin's City Portraits', p. 26.

51 Jacob Taubes, 'Culture and Ideology (1969)' in *From Cult to Culture: Fragments towards a Critique of Historical Reason* (Charlotte Elisheva Fonrobert and Amir

as Jürgen Habermas will a few years later, the anarchic traits in Benjamin's conception of society and law, Taubes raises questions about the concept of 'total mediation', which Adorno opposes to Benjamin's immediatism. Taubes contests the validity of Adorno's analysis of late capitalism.

> Also if one grants to Adorno that in the late capitalist epoch the abstraction of exchange value is not socially neutral [. . .] the question remains as to whether the gears, gnashing and groaning with untold victims, preserve themselves to this day 'only by means of profit interest'. Should the analysis of industrial society not be situated closer to the space of naked violence's madness and veiled domination than Adorno ventures? Is the law of exchange not overextended as a universal category for conceptualizing the constellation of the era of technology and industry, if profit-motive subjectively regresses and no longer objectively appears in an unmediated, clearly recognizable form as it does in the epoch of classical capitalism?[52]

The first long wave in the evaluation of Benjamin's thought came to an end that intersected with its powerful resonance during the student movement of 1968.[53] A new, fundamental phase in the critical literature on Benjamin was signalled in 1972 with the publication of a volume celebrating the eightieth anniversary of his birth,[54] including in particular Jürgen Habermas's essay 'Consciousness-Raising or Redemptive Criticism—The Contemporaneity of Walter Benjamin'.[55] Habermas starts

---

Engel eds) (Stanford, CA: Stanford University Press, 2009), pp. 248–67. See also 'Walter Benjamin—A Modern Marcionite?: Scholem's Benjamin Interpretation Reexamined' in Colby Dickinson and Stéphane Symons (eds), *Walter Benjamin and Theology* (New York: Fordham University Press, 2016), pp. 164–78.

52 Jacob Taubes, 'Culture and Ideology (1969)', p. 254.

53 On the relation between Benjamin and the movement of 1968, See Elvio Fachinelli, 'Quando Benjamin non ebbe "più niente da dire"', *Quaderni piacentini* 1 (1981): 81–93.

54 Siegfried Unseld (ed.), *Zur Aktualität Walter Benjamin* (Frankfurt am Main: Suhrkamp, 1972).

from the observation of the impossibility of reducing Benjamin's position to perspectives such as the one maintained, in the field of aesthetics, by Herbert Marcuse. In contrast to Marcuse, Benjamin is not moved by the demand for a critique of ideology. 'Marcuse confronts ideal and reality and raises to consciousness the unconscious content of bourgeois art, which both legitimates and unintentionally denounces bourgeois reality. Benjamin's analysis, on the other hand, dispenses with the form of self-reflection.'[56] Habermas highlights how Benjamin's thought rejects the tradition of idealist speculation but also its materialist opposite. Instead, Habermas sees in Benjamin's work an impulse to safeguard precisely that which is being critiqued.

> His critique of art approaches its objects in conservative fashion [. . .] It aims, it is true, at 'the mortification of the works', but the critique commits such destruction only in order to transpose what is worth knowing from the medium of the beautiful into that of truth—and thereby to rescue and redeem it.[57]

This impulse towards redemption has, furthermore, a precise correspondence in Benjamin's concept of history. Benjamin's redemptive attitude displays itself especially, Habermas argues, in its ambivalence towards the past.

> Benjamin's attitude towards the loss of aura was always ambivalent. Since the historical experience of a past *Jetztzeit* needs to be recharged, and because this experience is locked within the aura of a work of art, the undialectical disintegration of the aura would mean the loss of this experience.[58]

---

55 Jürgen Habermas, 'Consciousness-Raising or Redemptive Criticism: The Contemporaneity of Walter Benjamin' (Philip Brewster and Carl Howard Buchner trans.), *New German Critique* 17 (1979): 30–59.

56 Habermas, 'Consciousness-Raising or Redemptive Criticism': 37.

57 Habermas, 'Consciousness-Raising or Redemptive Criticism': 37.

58 Habermas, 'Consciousness-Raising or Redemptive Criticism': 44.

In this sense, Habermas stresses the presence in Benjamin's thought of two dialectically interwoven aspects: on the one hand, there is the awareness that in the course of its de-ritualization and loss of aura, the artwork also loses its experiential content, ending in banality; on the other, there is the opposing demand by which, with the loss of aura, esoteric experiences connected to the experience of happiness can for the first time become public and universal. Habermas finds the foundations of this ambivalent dialectic in the attitude towards the past—that is, the mythic tradition—that marks Benjamin's fundamentally mimetic conception of language.

> Benjamin was thinking of the semantic potential from which human beings draw and with which they invest the world with meaning, permitting it to be experienced. This semantic potential is deposited in myth to begin with and must be released from it—but it cannot be expanded, only continually transformed.[59]

Benjamin's worry in this regard is that in the course of this transformation, such semantic-mimetic energies might disperse and be lost to humanity. By carrying out this re-evaluation of the salvific impulse that animates Benjamin's philosophy of language and history, Habermas criticizes the negative position of Adorno towards this conservative tendency, which is in fact the essential force of Benjamin's thought.

> Adorno justifiably disapproves of this terminology. Yet he incorrectly maintains that the disenchantment of the dialectical image would of necessity lead back to purely mythical thought. Because the archaic in modernity, which Adorno sees more readily as being Hell than the Golden Age, contains precisely those possibilities of experience that point ahead to the utopian state of liberated society.[60]

---

59 Habermas, 'Consciousness-Raising or Redemptive Criticism': 47.

60 Habermas, 'Consciousness-Raising or Redemptive Criticism': 52.

Coherent with such a premise, Habermas also identified in Benjamin's political attitude something different from the acquiescence that Adorno reproaches him for in regards to traditional Marxism. Starting from an original reading of the essay 'Toward the Critique of Violence', Habermas instead sees an anarchic attitude which is the reversal of the idea of salvation and conservation. It isn't by chance, Habermas observes, that Benjamin, 'should refer to Sorel's myth of a general strike and to an anarchistic praxis which is distinguished by its banning of the instrumental character of action from the realm of political praxis and its negation of purposive rationality in favour of a "politics of pure means".'[61]

Starting in the 1970s, important contributions both to philosophy and to the interpretation of Benjamin's work have come from Giorgio Agamben, curator of the Italian edition of Benjamin's *Works*. In the essay entitled 'The Prince and the Frog' from his 1978 book *Infancy and History*, Agamben takes up an original and innovative position on the dispute between Adorno and Benjamin concerning the first draft of the essay on Baudelaire. Agamben points out the excessive zeal with which Adorno leapt in to accuse Benjamin of a 'vulgar materialism' that crossed magic with positivism. By so doing, Agamben observes, Adorno is dependent on a Hegelian conception, vindicating the idea of 'total mediation'. 'The mediator interposing its good offices between structure and superstructure to safeguard materialism from vulgarity, therefore, is Hegelian dialectical historicism, which, like all go-betweens, is prompt in demanding its percentage.'[62] Against Adorno's reading, Agamben makes it clear that Benjamin, like Marx, understood 'the relationship between structure and superstructure can neither be one of causal determination nor one of dialectical mediation, but one of direct correspondence.'[63] From this important clarification of the meaning of Benjamin's late orientation, Agamben was able to derive an important conclusion:

---

61 Habermas, 'Consciousness-Raising or Redemptive Criticism': 55.

62 Giorgio Agamben, *Infancy and History: The Destruction of Experience* (Liz Heron trans.) (London: Verso, 1993), p. 118.

63 Agamben, *Infancy and History*, p. 120.

> The statement 'the structure is the superstructure' is not just a deterministic proposition in the causal sense; it is not even a dialectical proposition in the ordinary sense, where, in place of the predicate, should be set the slow process of negation and of the *Aufhebung*. It is a speculative proposition—that is to say, immobile and immediate. This is the meaning of the 'dialectic at a standstill' which Benjamin leaves as a legacy to historical materialism, and with which it must reckon sooner or later.[64]

Jacques Derrida's important essay, 'Des tours de Babel', first published in the Italian journal *Aut-Aut* in 1982, follows Habermas in taking up the question of language in Benjamin. Discussing Benjamin's 'The Task of the Translator' and 'On Language as Such and on the Language of Man', Derrida investigates the motives that have led to the fragmentation of human experience and history. It was the will to power, with its arrogant nihilism, that substituted the immediacy of the divine word with infinitely scattered human speech, the Babel of languages, which exist now in continuous need of reciprocal translation. Following Benjamin's footsteps, Derrida discerns in translation a work of redemption; translation, that is, as an incessant re-composition of the originary divine language. This is similar to what Benjamin, in the realm of his philosophy of history, identified as the concept of 'now-time' (*Jeztzeit*). This task is accompanied, however, by the unawareness of the irremediability of the Fall. It is thus an effort characterized by permanence, by unceasingness, by the consciousness of being infinite and subject to the risk of betrayal and misrepresentation. Translation 'does not reproduce, does not restitute, does not represent; as to the essential, it does not render the meaning of the original except at that point of contact or caress, the infinitely small of meaning. It extends the body of languages, it puts languages into symbolic expansion.'[65] This symbolic expansion is the fruit of unending labour leading to fraternization among languages, a compensation for the destruction of Babel.

---

64 Agamben, *Infancy and History*, p. 123.

65 Jacques Derrida, 'Des Tours de Babel' in *Difference in Translation* (Joseph F. Graham ed. and trans.) (Ithaca, NY: Cornell University Press, 1985), p. 190.

> Through each language something is intended which is the same and yet which none of the languages can attain separately [. . .] What is intended, then, by this co-operation of languages and intentional modes is not transcendent to the language [. . .] What they are aiming at intentionally, individually and jointly, in translation is the language itself as a Babelian event, a language that is not the universal language in the Leibnizian sense, a language which is not the natural language that each remains on its own either; it is the being-language of the language, tongue or language as such, that unity without any self-identity, which makes for the fact that there are languages and that they are languages.[66]

The most recent stage of Benjamin criticism[67] has been produced largely in university settings, focused on plumbing specific issues in his work. For the amplitude of its theoretical breadth and its non-academic character, the studies dedicated to Benjamin's thought by Stéphane Mosès stand out in particular. In 'L'idée d'origine chez Walter Benjamin', published in 1983, Mosès demonstrates how the idea of origin, central to Benjamin's thought, is fuelled both by the biblical myth of the language of paradise and by Goethean morphology. It is thus marked by the primordial source of any knowledge, while also indicating a form capable of deciphering experience. History, which tends in Benjamin to move between the extremes of origin and utopia, is at the same time a catastrophic rupture of the first truth and an ever-renewing attempt to re-actualize, as Goethe would have it, the virtualities inscribed in the original. Like Derrida, Mosès shows how the conception of Benjamin's philosophy of history has its paradigm in the conception of language as presented in particular in the essay on the 'Task of the Translator'.

> Adamic language, defined by the perfect complementarity of signifier and signified, had disappeared in the moment when the word degraded into a simple instrument of communication;

66 Derrida, 'Des Tours de Babel', p. 201.

67 Note that Carchia's text was first drafted in 1971, and revised in 1999. [Trans.]

> the multiplicity of signifiers had covered up the semantic unicity of which each of the 'original names' was the bearer. History then appears as the process through which the broken perfection of adamic language reconstructs itself, thanks to the work of purification of language that translation and commentaries carry out on the body of the great literary texts. At the ideal end of this process—which is to say one never to be achieved—the original state of language must be restored and knowledge must return to its original integrity.[68]

No less important, also by Mosès, is the essay 'Walter Benjamins Kritik der historischen Vernunft' (1991). Here Mosès reveals Benjamin's transformation of the aesthetic paradigm delineated in the essay on *The Origin of German Tragic Drama* into a constellation of political categories. 'Critique of the temporal *continuum*, critique of historical causality, critique of the ideology of progress: through these three theses, his theological-political work disintegrates to its foundations the positivist conception of history.'[69] Benjamin opposes the positivist concept of historical reason with the power of memory, capable of undermining the irreversibility of historical judgement and thus the direction of history itself.

> Benjamin offers a consideration of history on the basis of which nothing would be forever sacrificed or lost. If every moment of the past can be re-actualized, can take place again in other conditions, on a new stage, then nothing in the history of humankind is irreparable. And, at the same time, nothing is inevitable in the future.[70]

---

68 Stéphane Mosès, 'L'idée d'origine chez Walter Benjamin' in Wismann (ed.), *Walter Benjamin et Paris*, pp. 809–26; here, p. 120. [In English, see Stéphane Mosès, *The Angel of History: Rosenzweig, Benjamin, Scholem* (Barbara Harshav trans.) (Stanford, CA: Stanford University Press, 1992), pp. 65–83 ('Metaphors of Origins: Ideas, Names, Stars'). —Trans.]

69 Stéphane Mosès, 'Walter Benjamins Kritik der historischen Vernunft', *Studi germanici* 29(83–85) (1991): 61–78; here, p. 61. [See Mosès, *The Angel of History*, pp. 10, 113. —Trans.]

70 Mosès, 'Walter Benjamins Kritik der historischen Vernunft': 77.

Bibliography

ADORNO, Theodor W. *Aesthetic Theory* (Gretel Adorno and Rolf Tiedmann eds, Robert Hullot-Kentor trans.). London: Continuum, 1997.

ADORNO, Theodor W. 'Charakteristik Walter Benjamin'. *Die Neue Rundschau* 61(4) (1950): 571–84.

ADORNO, Theodor W. 'Einleitung zu Benjamins Schriften' in *Walter Benjamin: Schriften*, VOL. 1 (Theodor W. Adorno and Gretel Adorno eds). Frankfurt am Main: Suhrkamp, 1955.

ADORNO, Theodor W. 'Erinnerung' in *Über Walter Benjamin* (Theodor W. Adorno, Ernst Bloch, Max Rychner, Gershom Scholem, Jean Selz, Hans Heinz Holz and Ernst Peter Fischer eds). Frankfurt am Main: Suhrkamp, 1968.

ADORNO, Theodor W. 'Introduction to Benjamin's *Schriften* (1955)' in Gary Smith (ed.), *On Walter Benjamin: Critical Essays and Recollections*. Cambridge, MA: MIT Press, 1988.

ADORNO, Theodor W. *Negative Dialectics* (E. B. Ashton trans.). London: Routledge, 1973.

ADORNO, Theodor W. 'A Portrait of Walter Benjamin' in *Prisms* (Samuel and Shierry Weber trans.). Cambridge, MA: MIT Press, 1981.

ADORNO, Theodor W. *Über Walter Benjamin*. Frankfurt am Main: Suhrkamp, 1970.

ADORNO, Theodor W. *Über Walter Benjamin*. Frankfurt am Main: Suhrkamp, 1990 [1970].

AGAMBEN, Giorgio. *Infancy and History: The Destruction of Experience* (Liz Heron trans.). London: Verso, 1993.

BARTHES, Roland. *On Racine* (Richard Howard trans.). New York: Performing Arts Journal Publications, 1983.

BENJAMIN, Walter. *Angelus Novus* (Renato Solmi trans.). Turin: Einaudi, 1962.

BENJAMIN, Walter. *The Arcades Project* (Rolf Tiedmann ed., Howard Eiland and Kevin McLaughlin trans). Cambridge, MA: Belknap Press, 2002.

BENJAMIN, Walter. *The Correspondence of Walter Benjamin, 1910–1940* (Manfred R. Jacobson and Evelyn M. Jacobson trans, Gershom Scholem and Theodor W. Adorno eds). Chicago, IL: University of Chicago Press, 1994.

BENJAMIN, Walter. *Das Passagen-Werk* (Rolf Tiedemann ed.), *Gesammelte Schriften*, VOL. 5, 2 PARTS. Frankfurt am Main: Surhkamp, 1982.

BENJAMIN, Walter. *Gesammelte Schriften*, 7 VOLS. Frankfurt am Main: Suhrkamp, 1972–1991.

BENJAMIN, Walter. *Illuminations* (Hannah Arendt ed., Harry Zohn trans.). New York: Schocken, 2007.

BENJAMIN, Walter. *The Origin of German Tragic Drama* (John Osborne trans., George Steiner intro.). London: Verso Books, 1998.

BENJAMIN, Walter. *Selected Writings*, 4 VOLS (Marcus Bullock, Michael W. Jennings, Howard Eiland and Gary Smith eds). Cambridge, MA: Harvard University Press, 1996–2003.

BENJAMIN, Walter, and Theodor W. Adorno. *The Complete Correspondence, 1928–1940* (Henri Lonitz ed., Nicholas Walker trans.). Cambridge, MA: Harvard University Press, 1999.

BROCH, Hermann. *Dichten und Erkennen, Gesammelte Werke*, VOL. 6. Zürich: Rhein Verlag, 1955.

BUBER, Martin. *Paths in Utopia* (R. F. C. Hull trans.). Boston: Beacon Press, 1958 [1949].

CASSIRER, Ernst. 'The Idea of Metamorphosis and Idealistic Morphology: Goethe' in *The Problem of Knowledge: Philosophy, Science and History since Hegel* (William H. Woglom and Charles W. Hendel trans). New Haven, CT: Yale University Press, 1950.

COHEN, Hermann. *System der Philosophie, Erster Teil: Logik der reinen Erkenntnis*. Berlin: Bruno Cassirer, 1914.

COOMARASWAMY, Ananda K. *The Transformation of Nature in Art*. New York: Dover, 1956[1934].

CROCE, Benedetto. *The Essence of Aesthetic* (Douglas Ainslie trans.). London: Heinemann, 1921.

DERRIDA, Jacques. 'Des Tours de Babel' in *Difference in Translation* (Joseph F. Graham trans. and ed.). Ithaca, NY: Cornell University Press, 1985.

DU BOS, Charles. *Che cos'è la letteratura*? Florence: Libreria Grandangolo, 1949.

DU BOS, Charles. 'L'ultimo amore di Goethe e l'elegia di Marienbad' in Johann Wolfgang Goethe, *Trilogia della passione* (Giovanna Bemporad trans.). Brescia: Morcelliana, 1952.

DU BOS, Charles. *What Is Literature*? London: Sheed and Ward, 1940.

FACHINELLI, Elvio. 'Quando Benjamin non ebbe "più niente da dire"'. *Quaderni piacentini* 1 (1981).

FOCILLON, Henri. *The Life of Forms in Art* (George Kubler trans.). Cambridge, MA: Zone Books, 1992.

FREUD, Sigmund. *New Introductory Lectures on Psycho-Analysis*. New York: Carlton House, 1933.

GARBER, Klaus. 'Étapes de la réception de Benjamin' in Heinz Wismann (ed.), *Walter Benjamin et Paris*. Paris: Cerf, 1986.

GARBER, Klaus. *Rezeption und Rettung*. Tübingen: Niemeyer, 1987.

GOETHE, Johann Wolfgang von. 'Reconciliation (Ein Gleichnis)', from 'Trilogy of Passion (1823–1824)' (John Frederick Nims trans.) in *Collected Works, Volume I: Selected Poems* (Christopher Middleton ed.). Princeton, NJ: Princeton University Press, 1994.

GOLDSTEIN, Kurt. 'L'analyse de l'aphasie et l'étude de l'essence du langage' in *Psychologie du langage*. Paris: Félix Alcan, 1933.

HABERMAS, Jürgen. 'Consciousness-Raising or Redemptive Criticism: The Contemporaneity of Walter Benjamin' (Philip Brewster and Carl Howard Buchner trans). *New German Critique* 17 (1979): 30–59.

HEGEL, Georg Wilhelm Friedrich. *The Phenomenology of Spirit* (Terry Pinkard ed. and trans.). Cambridge: Cambridge University Press, 2018.

HOLZ, Hans Heinz. 'Prismatisches Denken' in *Über Walter Benjamin* (Theodor W. Adorno, Ernst Bloch, Max Rychner, Gershom Scholem, Jean Selz, Hans Heinz Holz and Ernst Peter Fischer eds). Frankfurt am Main: Suhrkamp, 1968.

HORKHEIMER, Max, and Theodor W. Adorno. *Dialectic of Enlightenment: Philosophical Fragments* (Gunzelin Schmid Noerr ed., Edmund Jephcott trans.). Stanford, CA: Stanford University Press, 2002.

IVERNEL, Philippe. 'De la métaphysique du langage à la politique marxiste'. *Le Monde*, 31 May 1969.

KLOSSOWSKI, Pierre. 'Letter on Walter Benjamin (1952)' (Christian Hite trans.). *Parrhesia* 19 (2014): 14–21.

KOSELLECK, Reinhart. *Futures Past: On the Semantics of Historical Time* (Keith Tribe trans.). New York: Columbia University Press, 2004.

KRACAUER, Siegfried. 'On the Writings of Walter Benjamin' in *The Mass Ornament: Weimar Essays* (Thomas Y. Levin trans. and ed.). Cambridge, MA: Harvard University Press, 1995.

KRAFT, Werner. 'Walter Benjamin hinter seinen Briefen'. *Merkur* 21(3) (1967).

KRAUS, Karl. *Beim Wort genommen*. Munich: Kösel Verlag, 1955.

KRAUS, Karl. *Die Sprach*. Munich: Kösel Verlag, 1954.

LUKÁCS, György. *Estetica*, 2 vols. Turin: Einaudi, 1970.

LUKÁCS, György. *Soul and Form* (John T. Sanders and Katie Terazakis eds, Anna Bostock trans.). New York: Columbia University Press, 2010.

LUKÁCS, György. *The Specificity of the Aesthetic*, VOL. 1 (Erik M. Bachman and Tyrus Miller eds, Erik M. Bachman trans.). Chicago: Haymarket, 2024.

MANN, Thomas. Introduction to Johann Wolfgang von Goethe, *The Permanent Goethe* (Thomas Mann ed.). New York: The Dial Press, 1948.

MOSÈS, Stéphane. *The Angel of History: Rosenzweig, Benjamin, Scholem* (Barbara Harshav trans.). Stanford, CA: Stanford University Press, 1992.

MOSÈS, Stéphane. 'L'idée d'origine chez Walter Benjamin' in Heinz Wismann (ed.), *Walter Benjamin et Paris*. Paris: Cerf, 1986.

MOSÈS, Stéphane. 'Walter Benjamins Kritik der historischen Vernunft'. *Studi germanici* 29(83–85) (1991): 61–78.

PROUST, Marcel. *Time Regained* (Stephen Hudson trans.). London: Chatto & Windus, 1931.

RAULET, Gerard. *Le caractère destructeur*. Paris: Flammarion, 1997.

SCHLEGEL, Friedrich. 'An Idyll of Idleness' in "*Lucinde*" *and the Fragments* (Peter Firchow trans. and intro.). Minneapolis, MN: University of Minnesota Press, 1971.

SCHLEGEL, Friedrich. *Philosophische Vorlesungen (1800–1807)* (Jean-Jacques Anstett ed.). Munich / Paderborn / Vienna: Schöningh, 1964.

SCHOLEM, Gershom. 'Walter Benjamin'. *Die Neue Rundschau* 76(1) (1965): 1–21.

SOMMER, Manfred. *Lebenswelt und Zeitbewusstein*. Frankfurt am Main: Suhrkamp, 1990.

SZONDI, Péter. 'Hope in the Past: On Walter Benjamin' (Harvey Mendelsohn trans.). *Critical Inquiry* 4(3) (1978): 491–506.

SZONDI, Péter. 'Walter Benjamin's City Portraits (1962)' (Harvey Mendelsohn trans.) in Gary Smith (ed.), *On Walter Benjamin: Critical Essays and Recollections*. Cambridge, MA: MIT Press, 1998.

TAUBES, Jacob. 'Culture and Ideology (1969)' in *From Cult to Culture: Fragments towards a Critique of Historical Reason* (Charlotte Elisheva Fonrobert and Amir Engel eds). Stanford, CA: Stanford University Press, 2009.

TAUBES, Jacob. 'Walter Benjamin—A Modern Marcionite?: Scholem's Benjamin Interpretation Reexamined' in Colby Dickinson and Stéphane Symons (eds), *Walter Benjamin and Theology*. New York: Fordham University Press, 2016.

TIEDEMANN, Rolf. *Studien zur Philosophie Walter Benjamin*. Frankfurt am Main: Suhrkamp, 1965.

UNSELD, Siegfried, ed. *Zur Aktualität Walter Benjamin*. Frankfurt am Main: Suhrkamp, 1972.